HADRIAN'S WALL

By the same author:

Neolithic Cultures of North Africa, 1959

History from the Earth, 1974

Hillforts of the Iron Age in England & Wales, 1976

Prehistoric Britain & Ireland, 1976

Castles & Fortifications in Britain & Ireland, 1977

JAMES FORDE·JOHNSTON

HADRIAN'S WALL

Michael Joseph · London

First published in Great Britain by
Michael Joseph Limited
52 Bedford Square
London WC1
1978

By arrangement with Book Club Associates

© 1977 by James Forde-Johnston

DESIGNED BY CRAIG DODD

Printed and Bound by
GPS (Print) Limited and R. J. Acford
Limited (Bookbinders)

ISBN 0 7181 1652 6

CONTENTS

I
INTRODUCTION

In AD 117 Publius Aelius Hadrianus became Emperor of the mighty Roman Empire. Within five years of his accession he was in Britain, the major objective of his visit being the reorganization of the northern frontier, the most northerly of the whole Roman Empire. The eventual result (by c AD 130) was a frontier defence system, the major visible remnant of the Roman occupation, which we know as Hadrian's Wall. But although the name is long established, the frontier system which Hadrian brought into being was much more than a mere wall, even one some seventy-three miles long, from Wallsend-on-Tyne in the east to Bowness-on-Solway in the west. When we speak of Hadrian's Wall we speak, in fact, of a whole, integrated system of defences, including a *glacis* (an outer defence), a ditch, the Wall itself, a series of sixteen forts, each housing between 500 and 800 men, a series of eighty smaller forts, called milecastles, a series of 158 towers or turrets, a military road, and a rearward earthwork running behind the Wall (known as the Vallum) which delineated the military zone within which the whole system stood.

This system was continued down the Cumbrian coast for another forty miles, although it now consisted of forts, milecastles and towers only, the continuous linking Wall being omitted here, presumably because there was a natural barrier in front, namely the sea. There was, in addition, a series of outpost forts to the north of the Wall, some of which were part of the original scheme devised by Hadrian. All of these features will be described in more detail in later chapters. Before this is done, however, a certain amount of background needs to be filled in, so that Hadrian's Wall can be seen in its proper place in both the history and geography of the Roman Empire.

The Growth of Rome and the Empire

Roman history can be divided into three main periods: in the first period Rome was ruled by kings, from a traditional foundation date of 753 BC until 510 BC; the second period was that of the Roman Republic, from 510 BC to 27 BC, during which, in fact, most of the Empire was acquired; the third period was the Roman Empire, from 27 BC onwards when the Republican form of government was replaced by rule under an Emperor, the first of whom was Augustus, the nephew of Julius Caesar.

The first period need not concern us much here. Rome was ruled by kings and under Etruscan domination until 510 BC when the Romans had had enough of both and expelled their rulers, resolving never to be ruled by kings again and setting up a republic. During this early period the Romans were surrounded by more powerful neighbours: the Etruscans to the north, mentioned already; the Greeks to the south in southern

Opposite: The Emperor Hadrian.

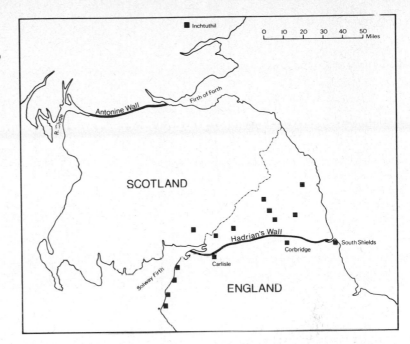

Italy and eastern Sicily (*Magna Graecia*); and the Carthaginians in North Africa and western Sicily. Much of the early history of Rome is concerned with struggles against these three powers and their eventual defeat.

In the early years of the Republic, the Romans had to fight for their existence, against the Etruscans among others, but they survived and gradually extended their own power and influence over neighbouring territories during the next two centuries. There was a severe setback in 390 BC when the Celtic tribes invaded Italy from the north and sacked Rome, but they eventually withdrew, suitably compensated. By c 300 BC Rome was in effective control of much of central Italy.

Shortly after this Rome came up against her first foreign foe, Pyrrhus, King of Epirus (in Greece), who landed in southern Italy in 280 BC. The outcome of the struggle was victory for Rome and the addition of the former Greek territories in southern Italy to the Roman domain. Victory in this area, however, brought her up against another enemy, the Carthaginians, who not only controlled western Sicily but also most of the trade in the western Mediterranean. The inevitable conflict of interest led to the first of the three Punic wars, from 264-241 BC, against what was probably Rome's most dangerous enemy in her early existence. The outcome was the withdrawal of the Carthaginians from Sicily which very soon became a Roman province, followed by Corsica and Sardinia. Additions in the north as far as the Po valley meant that already by 218 BC the city-state of Rome had acquired a considerable empire, consisting of most of Italy, plus Sicily, Sardinia and Corsica.

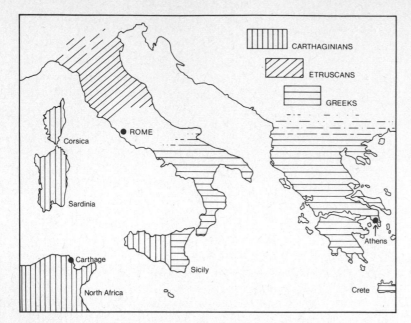

The central Mediterranean in the fourth century BC. During her early existence Rome was surrounded by three main enemies: the Greeks to the east, the Etruscans to the north, and the Carthaginians to the south and west.

The peace between Carthage and Rome from 241 to 218 BC was an uneasy one, each side aware that the other would be a permanent threat to its existence unless eliminated. War broke out again in 218 BC (the second Punic War), and during it emerged the greatest of the Carthaginian leaders, Hannibal, who came very close to complete victory over the Romans. Hannibal led his army through Spain, across the Pyrenees, and across the Alps into Italy where he stayed for fourteen years. The Romans suffered a severe defeat at Cannae in 216 BC, but they survived and continued the struggle. Gradually the tide turned. Hannibal's brother, Hasdrubal, brought in a fresh army in 207 BC but the Romans won a victory at the River Metaurus and Hasdrubal was killed. Hannibal withdrew to North Africa but the Romans now carried the war into Carthaginian territory and the second Punic war was over. One of the results was the addition of Spain to the growing list of Rome's possessions.

In spite of the victory, however, many Romans were still very suspicious of Carthage and felt that it ought to be completely destroyed to remove any possible threat for ever. Eventually, when Carthage looked as if her power might revive, the Romans found an excuse for attack and moved again into North Africa. At last, in 146 BC, Carthage was completely destroyed and Rome acquired a new province, in north-west Africa, and a foothold on a new continent. Around the same time Macedonia (167 BC) and Greece (146 BC) were acquired and this began a process of expansion in the east which, during the next century or so, was to produce an empire embracing the eastern end of the Mediterranean as completely as that at the western end.

For the purposes of this book it is events in western Europe which are of the greatest interest. Southern Gaul was acquired in 122 BC, and during the following century came the conquest of Gaul as a whole by Julius Caesar, described in his account, *De Bello Gallico* (literally, *About the Gallic War*), in the years between 58 and 50 BC. Caesar's advance in Gaul brought him up to the Channel coast, with only a short but—as he was to find out to his cost—dangerous sea crossing between him and what was to the Romans the mysterious island of Britain. With Gaul apparently under control and with the temptation of further prestige, Caesar made two forays into Britain in the years 55 and 54 BC. This was not the permanent conquest, as is so often assumed; such was not to come for another century, under the Emperor Claudius in AD 43. After 54 BC Caesar withdrew, having achieved his limited aims, and returned to complete the conquest of Gaul. Subsequently he returned to Rome, with his army, precipitating a civil war, from which he emerged as victor in 48 BC, and then ruled Rome for four years until he was assassinated in 44 BC.

Although Julius Caesar's invasions fell far short of complete conquest and were, in fact, little more than reconnaissances in depth, they had a number of important results for Britain's future. First of all, they brought Britain to Rome's attention and made the future conquest almost inevitable. They showed that the Channel crossing was an obstacle that could be overcome; only the particular circumstances to set the act of conquest in motion were now required. Perhaps of even greater importance were the consequences in the economic field. Trade links were now established and developed rapidly, producing wealth and a taste for Roman luxuries, such as wine, jewellery and silverware. Britain by this time was changing from a tribal society into a country of small kingdoms, some about the size of a county, others perhaps the size of several counties. Much of the wealth generated by trade was in the hands of the kings, princes and ruling houses of these kingdoms, further emphasizing the change in the social pattern. Inevitably, the Roman way of life became the standard to aim for and some kingdoms established contacts with Rome at a diplomatic level. A squabble between two of these kingdoms in southern England was followed by an appeal from one of them to Rome for assistance, and this provided the excuse for Roman intervention and the subsequent conquest of Britain in AD 43. This, however, was only the pretext and not the basic reason, and to understand the latter it is necessary to return, briefly, to events in Rome following the assassination of Julius Caesar in 44 BC.

The death of Caesar was followed by a long civil war, won eventually by his nephew Octavianus who, in 27 BC, became the first Emperor, taking the name of Augustus, and establishing the Caesars as the ruling dynasty for almost a

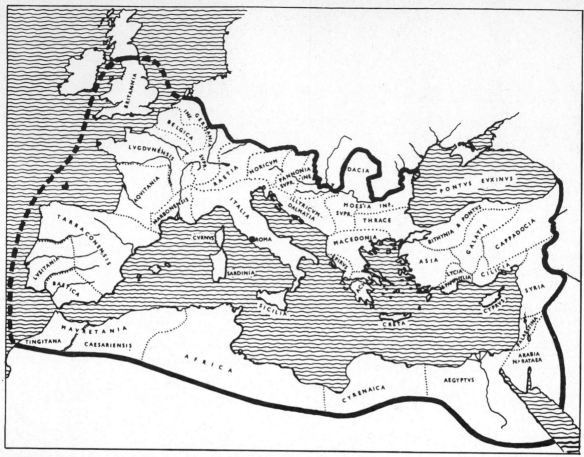

century (27 BC–AD 68). During this period further additions were made to the already extensive Empire built up in the Republican period, mostly in Asia and eastern Europe. In northern Europe the attempt to establish the frontier on the river Elbe in the time of Augustus was given up when three legions were cut to pieces by German tribes, and the frontier eventually settled on the Rhine-Danube line, from the North Sea to the Black Sea.

Augustus died in AD 14 and was succeeded by his stepson, Tiberius, who, in fact, had borne the brunt of much of the fighting in Germany. Tiberius ruled for twenty-three years (AD 14-37), and was succeeded briefly by Caligula (AD 37-41), who, it is generally agreed, was mad. Caligula, in turn, was succeeded by Claudius (AD 41-54), and it was during his reign that the invasion of Britain took place and the long process of conquest began. Why it took place has little to do with any desire to intervene in a squabble between two petty kingdoms on the outer fringes of the Roman Empire. A number of factors were involved. There was the natural desire of Claudius, early in his reign, to achieve the prestige of a military success and an addition to the Empire. Apart from Caligula, whose reign was too short to count, his predecessors

The map of the Roman Empire shows very clearly the enormous extent of its frontiers in Africa, Asia and Europe. In Europe the frontier was based largely on the Rhine and the Danube although in certain periods it was pushed beyond these natural barriers.

Opposite: The Emperor Claudius (AD 41-54). It was under Claudius that the occupation of Britain began in AD 43, although the final conquest took another forty years to complete.

14

as Emperor, Augustus and Tiberius, both had considerable military achievements to their credit, and in order to put himself on the same level Claudius needed some comparable achievement. Britain seemed ready made, and after centuries of steady expansion the addition of another province must have seemed the most natural process in the world. The fact that one of his ancestors, Julius Caesar, had visited the island twice and exacted tribute must have made the invasion seem like the completion of a Roman task already long begun.

There was, in addition, one more practical reason for bringing Britain into the Empire. The Gallic tribes conquered by Caesar between 58 BC and 50 BC were Celts, like the tribes in most of central and western Europe, including Britain. Although Gaul as a whole was pacified by Caesar there were still, from time to time, uprisings against Roman rule, particularly in the north, which needed to be put down. Often, however, when Roman retribution was imminent the tribesmen involved were able to escape across the Channel to southern Britain where they could find refuge among sympathetic cousins. The desire to close this back door could be added to the reasons already mentioned to make up a fairly convincing case for the conquest of Britain and its inclusion in the Roman Empire.

The Conquest of Britain

Having decided on invasion Claudius chose Aulus Plautius to be the general in charge and gave him four legions, the Second Augusta, the Ninth Hispana, the Fourteenth Gemina and the Twentieth Valeria Victrix, together with a considerable force of auxiliary troops. The four legions amounted to between 20,000 and 25,000 men and the auxiliary troops may have increased this to a total army of between 40,000 and 50,000 men. The main landing and main supply base were at Richborough in Kent, but there were simultaneous landings at Dover and Lympne to broaden the front. The main British resistance was led by the two sons of King Cunobelinus (Shakespeare's Cymbeline), Togidumnus and Caratacus. The first major clash came on the river Medway in the region of the present-day Rochester. The two-day battle was won by the Romans and Togidumnus was killed. The Britons retreated to the north-west and were defeated again on the Thames in the area of what was to become *Londinium* (Roman London).

With the crossing of the Thames secured, the way to the local native capital, *Camulodunum* (modern Colchester), lay open. This seemed an appropriate time to bring the Emperor over to enjoy his triumph and enter the enemy capital as victor. Accordingly Aulus Plautius waited until Claudius arrived from Rome to take charge during the last week or two of the initial campaign. Although not much was demanded of

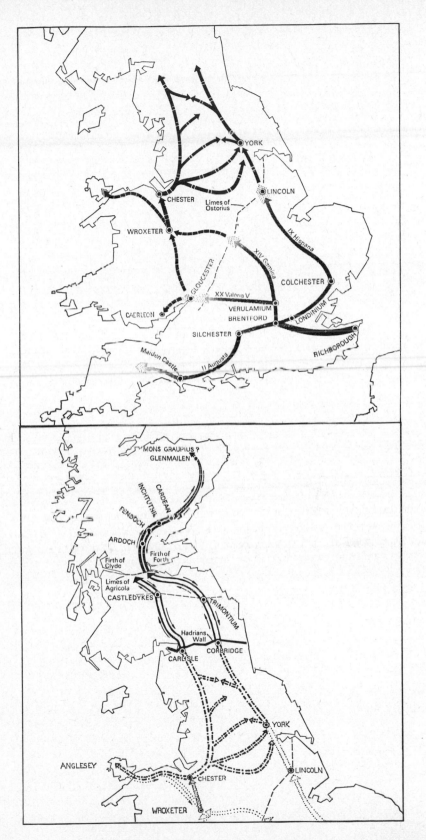

Map illustrating the progress of the conquest, AD 43-71: AD 43, invasion; AD 47, Severn-Trent frontier; AD 47-51, campaign in South Wales and defeat of Caratacus; AD 61, campaign in North Wales and Boudiccan revolt; AD 71, beginning of campaign to subdue the Brigantes in the north of England.

Map illustrating the later stages of the conquest: AD 78, the arrival of Agricola as governor; AD 79, completion of Brigantian conquest; AD 80, establishment of Stanegate line; AD 81, Lowland conquest; AD 83, invasion of Highlands; AD 84, battle of Mons Graupius and recall of Agricola; AD 86-100, withdrawal from Scotland and return to Stanegate line; AD 122, Hadrian's visit to Britain and the beginning of the Wall.

him in the circumstances Claudius, nevertheless, seems to have led the army quite capably, winning a pitched battle and pushing the natives back in the direction of Colchester which he eventually entered in triumph. The fall of Colchester brought about the collapse of resistance in much of south-eastern England and the first stage of the conquest was over, although the remaining stages were to take considerably longer, being spread over some forty years.

After sixteen days Claudius departed for Rome, having achieved his objective of a military triumph and an addition to the Empire. Although everything had gone according to plan Claudius left behind one enemy as yet undefeated, Caratacus. When he realised that further resistance in the south-east was useless Caratacus fled west into Wales where he carried on a stubborn resistance for another nine years. He eventually fell into Roman hands in AD 51, handed over to them by Cartimandua, queen of the Brigantes of northern England, to whom he had fled after being defeated in North Wales. He was sent captive to Rome with his family where Claudius, impressed by his pride and courage, showed clemency, and allowed him to end his days in honourable captivity, probably aided with a small pension. He never returned to Britain.

From the south-east the conquest proceeded in three directions, north, north-west and west, still under the generalship of Aulus Plautius who resumed control again after the departure of Claudius. He sent the Ninth Legion northwards, eventually into Leicestershire. The Fourteenth and Twentieth Legions went north-west into the Midlands, while the Second went westwards into Dorset and Wiltshire. The commander in the west was Vespasian, who, some twenty-five years later, was to become Emperor himself (in AD 69), ending the period of confusion which followed the death of Nero, last of the Caesars, in AD 68. Vespasian is recorded as capturing twenty *oppida* and these must be the native hillforts, including the well-known Maiden Castle, in Dorset, which were the chief points of resistance against the Roman advance.

Aulus Plautius stayed for four years as governor (until AD 47), and was succeeded by Ostorius Scapula. By this time there was a (temporary) north-east/south-west frontier on the line of the rivers Trent and Severn. Under Ostorius Scapula the Ninth Legion moved forward from Leicester to Lincoln, the Fourteenth and Twentieth to Wroxeter in Shropshire, and the Second from Gloucester to Caerleon. The latter proved the focus of resistance in South Wales where the Silures, led by Caratacus, were particularly troublesome. Ostorius Scapula moved against them in force and forced Caratacus to retreat to the north where he was eventually defeated somewhere on the Severn and fled to Brigantian territory, with the consequences described earlier. In spite of this defeat,

however, Welsh resistance, aided by the difficult terrain, continued for several more decades.

In AD 59 a new governor, Suetonius Paulinus, was appointed. His first objective was to complete the conquest of North Wales, and particularly Anglesey, the great stronghold of the Druidic religion which was, in fact, one of the major reasons for the long and stubborn resistance put up by the Welsh. After careful preparation, including the building of boats, Paulinus moved into North Wales and advanced to somewhere in the Bangor area, with only the narrow straits between him and Anglesey. The Ordovices, the people of North Wales, had gathered on the island to defend their sanctuaries and faced the Romans on the far shore. Already equipped with boats the Romans crossed in force and defeated the waiting tribesmen. This should have been the end of Welsh resistance, but in the moment of victory Paulinus received news of a serious revolt in eastern Britain which had been quiet for ten years. The events of AD 61 were to delay the final conquest of North Wales for another two decades.

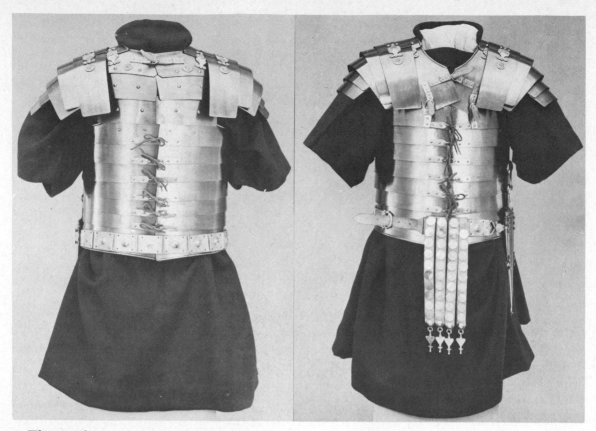

The revolt was led by Boudicca (Boadicea), queen of the Iceni, the people of Norfolk and Suffolk, one of the small British kingdoms referred to earlier. In AD 61 Boudicca's husband, King Prasutagus, died, leaving half of his possessions and kingdom to Rome. Unfortunately, Roman officials seized more than they were entitled to under the terms of the will and so outraged the Iceni that they rose in armed revolt. They were probably encouraged in their decision to resist by the knowledge that the governor was heavily engaged far away in North Wales. They were joined by the Trinovantes, the people of Essex, who still resented having lost land in the time of Ostorius Scapula to establish a *colonia* at Camulodunum (Colchester); a *colonia* is a settlement specially built for retired legionary soldiers (*veterani*), and Colchester was the first truly Roman town built in Britain.

The rebels captured and destroyed Camulodunum and then turned on the one legion left in the east, the Ninth, at Lincoln, commanded by Petilius Cerialis, who was to become governor himself some years later. The legion was badly mauled, losing some 2,000 men, nearly half its total strength. These early successes were encouraging and most of the surrounding tribes now joined the revolt. The Romans and their British supporters fled and sought refuge in the two principal towns of the province, *Londinium* (London) and *Verulamium* (St

Above: Roman legionary helmet. The peak-like projection was, in fact, worn at the back and was designed to protect the back of the neck. The pieces at the sides (cheek-pieces) were intended to protect the sides of the face.

Opposite: Roman body armour (lorica segmentata, Corbridge Type A). An important find of Roman armour at Corbridge about ten years ago made possible a virtually complete reconstruction of this piece of equipment. Reconstruction by H. Russell Robinson.

Albans). This was the situation when news of the revolt reached Paulinus in Anglesey, with final victory over the Welsh within his grasp.

Paulinus turned away from North Wales and headed for the south-east and the heart of the revolt. He gathered together the Fourteenth and Twentieth legions on the way and sent orders for the Second legion (at Caerleon) to join him. When he reached London and was able to make his own assessment of the situation he realised that the city, as yet without walls, would be difficult to defend. He decided to keep his forces intact and for the moment to retreat to the west, accompanied no doubt by the people who had taken refuge in the two cities. This left the rebels with a free hand and they thereupon captured and burned both *Londinium* and *Verulamium*.

Flushed with success the rebels turned west in pursuit of Paulinus, no doubt hoping to destroy his forces completely. But he retreated in good order, keeping his army intact and awaiting his opportunity to strike back. The rebels, over-confident and slowed down by booty, including livestock, also lacked discipline and organization. At a time and place of his own choosing Paulinus turned and faced the following rebel horde and completely defeated them. Boudicca fled and committed suicide. The Romans then embarked on a savage punitive campaign, laying waste to the land and possessions of the rebel tribes. So severe were the measures adopted by Paulinus that they were in danger of provoking further trouble in the future. The *procurator* (the senior treasury official in Britain) saw that more conciliatory methods might bring better dividends in the long run and so advised the Emperor. Paulinus, his main task complete, was recalled and a new governor appointed.

One of the results of the events of AD 61 was a sustained campaign of Romanization in the south-east over the next ten years, and this area never again gave trouble during the whole Roman occupation. In AD 71 Petilius Cerialis, former commander of the Ninth Legion at Lincoln, was appointed governor of Britain. Much of his time was taken up with northern England (*Brigantia*) where a civil war had turned a former friendly state into a hostile one. Without achieving complete conquest he nevertheless penetrated deeply into Brigantian territory and made Agricola's task very much easier (below). As part of his effort he moved the northern legionary base from Lincoln to York (*Eburacum*) where it was to remain for the next three centuries or more. Lincoln later became a *colonia* for retired legionary veterans. Cerialis was succeeded in AD 74 by Sextus Julius Frontinus. During his term of office (AD 74-78) there was an outbreak of trouble among the Silures of South Wales. Frontinus defeated them and planted a series of forts throughout their territory. After some thirty years of resistance they finally accepted defeat at his

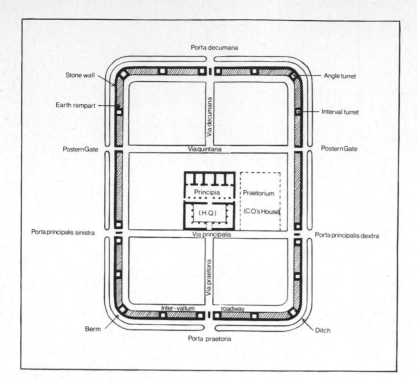

Porta decumana

Stone wall

Angle turret

Earth rampart

Interval turret

Via decumana

Postern Gate

Via quintana

Postern Gate

Principia

Praetorium

(H.Q)

(C.O.'s House)

Porta principalis sinistra

Via principalis

Porta principalis dextra

Via praetoria

Inter-vallum   roadway

Berm

Ditch

Porta praetoria

Layout and terminology of Roman fortifications. Roman legionary fortresses and auxiliary forts were built to a standard plan, based largely on the layout of internal roads: the via praetoria, *the* via principalis, *the* via quintana *and the* via decumana.

hands, and from then on gave no serious trouble to the Romans.

In AD 78 Cnaeus Julius Agricola was appointed governor of Britain. We know a great deal about him because he was the father-in-law of the Roman historian Tacitus who wrote his biography (*The Agricola*). Agricola knew Britain already, having previously been on the staff of Suetonius Paulinus when he defeated Boudicca and later when he was appointed *legatus* (i.e. commander) of the Twentieth Legion.

Agricola arrived in Britain again in midsummer AD 78 and immediately turned his attention to one of the problems of Britain, outstanding since AD 61, when Suetonius Paulinus had been forced by events elsewhere to leave his work in Anglesey uncompleted. He moved against the Ordovices of North Wales, defeated them, and pressed on to Anglesey. It was now late in the season for campaigning and there were no ships available. It would have been easy to defer any further action until the following year but Agricola was determined to continue. A special force of auxiliary cavalry swam their horses across the straits and this was the end of resistance by the Ordovices, seventeen years after the original crossing (in boats) by Paulinus. They sued for peace and thereafter there was no further trouble from Wales. Nevertheless, the Romans were taking no chances and the country was now secured by a network of fortifications consisting of two legionary fortresses, one at Chester (*Deva*), and one at Caerleon (*Isca*), and a whole series of smaller auxiliary forts scattered throughout Wales.

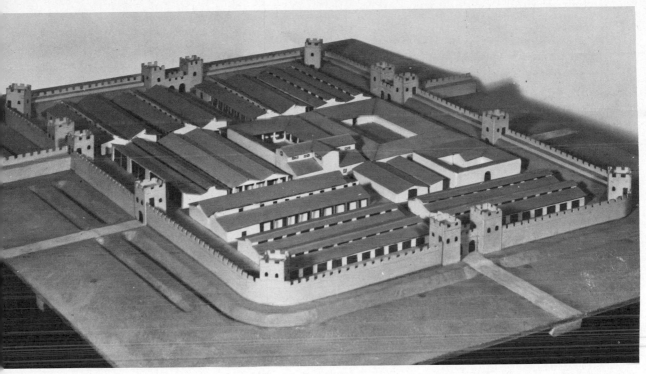

Model of a Roman auxiliary fort.

Together with York, Chester and Caerleon became the three permanent legionary bases in Britain during the next three centuries.

The subjugation of the Ordovices meant that all of England and Wales south of a line from Chester to York was now secure. Agricola's ambition, however, and indeed the Roman intention, must have been to conquer the whole island of Britain—i.e., Scotland as well as England and Wales. But to do this Agricola first had to finish off the work begun by Cerialis in the north of England among the Brigantes, probably the most troublesome of Rome's enemies in Britain. The details of the campaign are not known, but within the next few years a series of forts in and around their territory indicate the establishment of Roman control although, as will be seen later, this was by no means the end of Brigantian resistance. For the purpose of this book the most significant aspect of Agricola's northern campaigns was the building of the Stanegate and the Stanegate forts, at the northern edge of Brigantian territory. The Stanegate was an east-west road from a fort at Corbridge (Northumberland) to one at Carlisle (Cumbria), with a series of forts in between, which formed a frontier very close to the line of the later Hadrian's Wall, and which was to play an important part in its conception. The Stanegate forts figure prominently in the planning of the Wall some forty years later.

For Agricola, however, the Stanegate frontier was only a stepping stone to Scotland. In AD 81 he moved into the

23

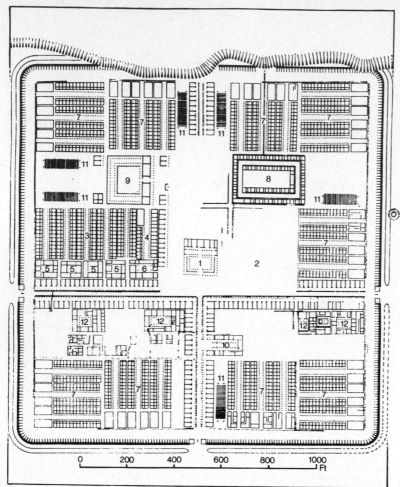

Plan of the legionary fortress at Inchtuthil. In spite of its size and elaborate plan Inchtuthil was abandoned within a few years of its original construction by the Governor Agricola (AD 78-84).
Key: 1. Headquarters; 2. site for commandant's house; 3. barrack accommodation for First Cohort; 4. accommodation for cavalry unit; 5. houses for centurions of First Cohort; 6. house for senior centurion, First Cohort; 7. groups of six barrack blocks, one group for each cohort; 8. hospital; 9. workshop; 10. drill hall; 11. granaries; 12. tribunes (officer's) houses.

Lowland zone and established another significant line of forts between the Clyde and the Forth, the line which the Antonine Wall was to follow some sixty years later. Here there was a pause while the advance was consolidated and active campaigning was resumed only in AD 83. In this year Agricola advanced up the east side of Highland Scotland, his route being marked by a line of forts, culminating in the legionary fortress of Inchtuthil (*Pinnata Castra*), in Tayside, the most northerly legionary base in the Roman Empire, and probably the shortest-lived, for Inchtuthil was abandoned within a few years of being built. In the following year (AD 84) Agricola pursued his advance and brought the Highland tribes to battle at Mons Graupius, a place as yet unidentified, but one which represented a great victory for the Romans. This left them firmly in control of Lowland Scotland, behind the Forth-Clyde line, with the Highland tribes beyond badly mauled and in no condition to make trouble for some considerable time to come. Whether this was the limit of Agricola's intentions or whether he planned to resume operations the following season we shall never know, for he was recalled to Rome by the Emperor Domitian (AD 81-96) during the winter of AD 84-85, his governorship at an end.

There is not much information about events during the next forty years, between Agricola's recall and Hadrian's visit to Britain in AD 122. The hold on Lowland Scotland seems to have been retained for some time, probably a decade or more, but at some stage, possibly *c* AD 100, all the Lowland forts seem to have been given up. Certainly by the time of Hadrian's accession (AD 117) the frontier was back on the Stanegate and may have been there already for some considerable time.

The reason for this contraction of Roman territory is uncertain. It may have been the result of pressure by Scottish tribes, still smarting from the defeat at Mons Graupius a generation before; it may have been trouble behind the frontier, among the Lowland tribes or the Brigantes; or it may have been the result of withdrawing military units from Britain for service elsewhere in the Empire, leaving the remaining forces too stretched for safety. Certainly we know that one legion, the Second Adiutrix, which had been in Britain only since AD 71, was withdrawn for service in Pannonia in central Europe in AD 86. This left Britain with only three legions, which was to be its permanent legionary complement from this time on. The Second Adiutrix had been stationed at Chester. To replace it the Twentieth Legion was withdrawn from Inchtuthil and remained at Chester for the next three centuries. This is almost certainly the reason for the abandonment of Inchtuthil so soon after it was built. A reduction of twenty-five per cent in the legionary strength (from four legions to three), must have brought about a searching re-appraisal of the whole military situation, particularly if some auxiliary units were withdrawn as well; and there is, indeed, evidence that under the Emperor Trajan (AD 98-117) some British auxiliary units were serving in Dacia (modern Rumania). The result of all these changes was probably a decision to withdraw, either immediately or progressively, to a position where the (reduced) forces available were adequate for the job in hand, and this, presumably, was judged to be the Stanegate line, originally established by Agricola in AD 80.

There is thus no doubt that by the time of Hadrian's accession (AD 117), the northern frontier of Britain was on the Stanegate line where it had been forty years previously, before Agricola's excursion into Scotland. There seems to have been trouble in Britain early in Hadrian's reign, probably in AD 117-118, although the details are far from clear. It is around this time that the Ninth Legion was transferred from Britain, to be replaced shortly afterwards by the Sixth which was to remain permanently at York. It used to be thought that the Ninth was wiped out in some disaster, or if not wiped out, was cashiered for disgraceful conduct, but there is now little doubt that it survived, and there are records of its existence in other parts of the Empire later in the century. It may, however, have been the events of AD 117-18 which, among other things, brought the Emperor to the province in AD 122, to initiate the building of Britain's most enduring Roman monument, Hadrian's Wall.

The Organization of the Roman Army

Before dealing with the Wall itself something must be said about the Roman army and its organization. Reference has been made already to legionary troops and auxiliary troops, and these two terms, and some others, need to be explained as part of the background to the study of Hadrian's Wall. The Roman army consisted of two main sections, the legions and the auxiliary units. The legions were composed of highly-trained troops, mostly heavy infantry, but with a small contingent of cavalry, all of them Roman citizens. These were the crack troops of the army and included a wide range of skills, enabling them to undertake a multitude of tasks in addition to fighting: surveying, building, engineering etc. The other section, the auxiliaries, were native troops raised localy in the various provinces of the Empire (Spain, North Africa, Syria, Britain etc.), with Roman officers but their own native weapons and equipment. The auxiliary units could be either infantry or cavalry or a combination of the two. As far as Hadrian's Wall is concerned, it was the legionary troops who built the Wall, while it was the auxiliary troops who provided the garrison to man it. Only in the legions could be found the skills necessary for so complex a building operation. On the other hand, such highly trained troops were not normally employed on frontier duties, so that once the Wall was complete it fell naturally to auxiliary units to take over and operate the system provided by the legions.

As their name indicates, the legionary troops were organized in legions, between 5,000 and 5,500 strong (roughly the equivalent of a division in modern military terms). At any one time there were about thirty legions in the Roman army, with an overall total of 150-160,000 men, although these were never available as a combined force. The legions were dispersed throughout the Empire in a series of permanent bases (three of them in Britain), and this dispersal was indeed an important part of Imperial policy. The concentration of too large a military force under an ambitious governor or general was always a potential threat to the throne, and indeed, as will be seen later, the existence of three legions in Britain (a tenth of the whole legionary force), together with the auxiliaries, proved too great a temptation on a number of occasions in the history of Roman Britain.

Each legion was divided into ten cohorts, of which the First Cohort was somewhat special. The other nine were divided into six centuries of eighty men each, so that each cohort contained 480 men. (Although the term century means literally a hundred, and presumably had originally consisted of a hundred men, by Hadrian's time the complement had been reduced to eighty, although the term century was retained from long usage). In charge of each century was a centurion and these were the backbone of the legionary system. There were thus in the nine cohorts 4,320 men. The First Cohort was larger than the others and consisted of double centuries (160 men), but had only five of them instead of the usual six, bringing the legionary complement up to 5,120. The addition of a small cavalry unit (c 120 men), of more senior officers, and of various specialists, probably brought the total up to c 5,300 or 5,350 men when the legion was at full strength.

The auxiliary troops were organized in much smaller groups, but obviously modelled on the legionary pattern. An auxiliary infantry unit consisted of a single cohort, either 480 strong (6 centuries) or 800 strong (10 centuries)—i.e., the same size as the two types of legionary cohort. The smaller cohorts are designated *quingenary* cohorts (i.e., nominally 500 strong), and the larger ones *milliary* (i.e., nominally 1,000), and both types will be encountered again when the Wall garrison is being considered.

In addition to infantry, the auxiliary forces also included cavalry units (*alae*), of generally similar sizes. These were divided into *turmae* of 32 men each, with 16 *turmae* in a *quingenary ala* (512 men and their horses), and 24 *turmae* in a *milliary ala* (768 men and their horses), although the latter type of formation is rather rare.

Besides the pure infantry and cavalry units there were also units which mixed the two (*cohors equitata*), again of both sizes, *quingenary* (probably 360 infantry and 120 cavalry), and *milliary* (probably 600 infantry and 240 cavalry). All three types of unit in both sizes were present in the garrison troops along the Wall.

Legions and auxiliary troops account for the bulk of the Roman army, but there is in fact, a third group. These can best be described as 'irregulars' and were probably hired *en masse* as mercenary troops, with their own chiefs or leaders. They appear occasionally in the Wall garrison in the third and fourth centuries. A unit of irregular infantry was known as a *numerus*, while a unit of irregular cavalry was called a *cuneus*.

Roman Fortresses and Forts

The careful organization of the legions and auxiliary troops was matched by the structures in which they were housed. The

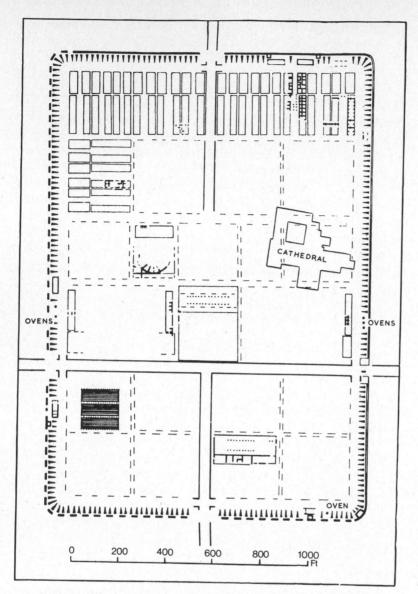

CATHEDRAL

OVENS

OVENS

OVEN

0   200   400   600   800   1000
                                  Ft

The legionary fortress at Chester (Deva). Although the plan is less complete than Inchtuthil the same general layout can be observed.

term fortress is usually reserved for legionary establishments, while the term fort is usually taken to indicate one for an auxiliary unit. The size of a legion, *c* 5,000 men, quite clearly called for something much larger than was required to house, say, an auxiliary cohort of 480 men, and legionary fortresses are in general about ten times the size of auxiliary forts. Legionary fortresses were, on average, fifty acres in area and this provided space for the barrack blocks, the headquarters, officers' houses, granaries, workshops etc. all laid out according to a regular formula which reflects the order and discipline of the Roman army. The same layout, allowing for the great difference in size, was followed also in the auxiliary forts.

In plan both legionary fortresses and auxiliary forts were

rectangular, with rounded corners, rather like the shape of a playing card. There were normally four entrances, one in each side, although some forts along the Wall had six. These entrances were linked with the internal road system which is the key to the whole Roman plan. One entrance, usually in one of the shorter sides, formed the principal gate of the fort or fortress and was known as the *porta praetoria*. This gave access to the *via praetoria* which led up to the headquarters building, the *principia*. This was always situated at the junction of the *via praetoria* and another road, *via principalis*, which ran across the fort between the entrances in the two long sides, forming a T-shaped arrangement which is a standard part of any Roman legionary fortress or auxiliary fort. Parallel to the *via principalis* was another road running across the site (the *via quintana*), and between them these two roads divided the interior into three sections. It was at the ends of this second road that the additional entrances (where they existed) were situated. A road at right angles (the *via decumana*), forming another T-shaped arrangement, led to the back gate of the fort, the *porta decumana*.

These internal arrangements were common to both the large legionary fortresses and the much smaller auxiliary forts, and provided the framework into which all the buildings required could be fitted. The location of one such building, the *principia* (headquarters) has been indicated already. Alongside the headquarters was the house of the commandant (the *praetorium*), whether it was the house of the *legatus* or general of a legion, or the house of a less senior officer, the tribune of an auxiliary unit. Both headquarters and commandant's house occupied the central sector between the *via principalis* and the *via quintana* and in general this sector contained all the buildings, other than the barrack blocks and stables, which a military camp called for. These for the most part were located in two remaining sectors, the front of the *via principalis* and to the rear of the *via quintana*.

The nature of legionary fortresses can be best understood by considering a specific example and one which has been mentioned already in connection with Agricola's campaigns in Scotland, Inchtuthil, in Tayside. The space to the east of the headquarters is vacant, but this is where the commandant's house would have been; presumably it had not been built when the site was abandoned. The space to the west provided the accommodation for the First cohort, the most senior in the legion, with double centuries, which normally occupied this privileged position. The other nine cohorts were accommodated in nine groups of barrack blocks (6 blocks to a group) which occupy much of the remaining space. Within each group the plan clearly shows the layout of the six barrack blocks, one for each century. Including those of the First cohort there were thus in all sixty-four barrack blocks. Other

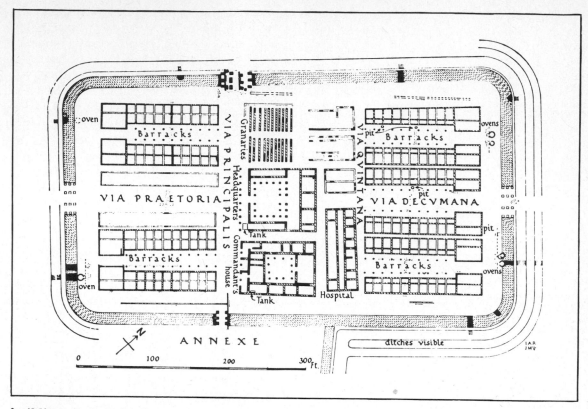

The plan shows a Roman fort with the following labels: oven, Barracks, VIA PRINCIPALIS, Granaries, Headquarters, Commandant's house, VIA PRAETORIA, Tank, Tank, Hospital, VIA QVINTANA, pit, Barracks, ovens, co, VIA DECVMANA, pit, Barracks, ovens, oven, ANNEXE, ditches visible, 0 100 200 300 Ft.

buildings included a hospital, a large workshop, a drill hall, six granaries, and numerous smaller structures, the functions of which are not always clear. There were also four more houses, for four of the six tribunes or officers which a legion normally had.

The plans of the three permanent legionary bases in Britain (Chester, York and Caerleon) are less complete than Inchtuthil, but as far as they are known they follow, with only minor variations, the same plan and internal layout.

As an example of an auxiliary fort, another work of Agricola in Tayside can be described, Fendoch. This has the four entrances and the same layout of roads, dividing the interior into three sections. In front of the *via principalis* were four barrack blocks and behind the *via quintana* were six more, so that the fort was designed to house a milliary cohort of 800 men. In the central sector were the headquarters building, the commandant's house, two granaries, a hospital and one or two smaller buildings, probably for storage or maintenance work. Although only a tenth of the size of a legionary fortress, the relationship between the two types of fortification is clear: the auxiliary fort is a scaled-down version of the legionary fortress.

In addition to legionary fortresses and auxiliary forts, there are two other, smaller types of military structure which are important to any understanding of the Wall. One of these,

Fendoch in Tayside was one of the auxiliary forts built by Agricola (AD 78-84) during his campaigns in Scotland. As with all fortifications of that period its defences were earthwork faced with timber and its internal buildings were timber-framed. Apart from this it bears a close resemblance to one of the best-known forts along the Wall, Housesteads, and like it, was designed to house a military or large cohort, of 800 men, (ten centuries) instead of the smaller cohort of 480 men (six centuries).

termed a fortlet, is a miniature version of an auxiliary fort, usually 80-100 feet square, still with the rounded corners, but now with a single entrance. The buildings inside usually consisted of one or two small barrack blocks on either side of a central roadway. Such fortlets were provided where there was a need for a small detachment, say fifty or sixty men, to be on duty in a particular place, such as an outpost from a larger fort, at a particular road junction or river crossing, or at an important signalling post. Fortlets occupy an important position in the range of structures involved in Hadrian's Wall, although under a different name, milecastles, which tends to obscure the fact that they are a standard type of Roman fortification and not something devised specially for the Wall.

The same is true of the second type, the tower, which appears along the Wall under the name of a turret. Free-standing towers, about 20 feet square, were another type of Roman military structure, often used as signal stations or watch towers, placed at suitable vantage points, for example between two forts to facilitate communication, or at the head of a mountain pass to give early warning of enemy movement.

Roman Frontier Defences

In addition to Hadrian's Wall, Britain possesses another elaborate frontier defence, the Antonine Wall, to be described later. These, however, are only two of a whole range of defence systems along the enormous frontier of the Roman Empire. Roman frontiers and their defences form a special subject of study and there is a regular 'Limes Congress' which meets in different parts of the former Roman Empire. Limes (pronounced lee-maze), can best be translated as 'the frontier and its attendant defence works', or simply 'the frontier'.

In Europe the frontier of the Roman Empire was substantially along the Rhine and the Danube, from Holland

The early third-century Roman frontier in south-west Germany consisted of a stone wall with stone watch-towers or turrets, very much on the lines of Hadrian's Wall. It was the work of the Emperor Caracalla (AD 211-217) who succeeded to the throne while he was in Britain when his father Septimus Severus died in York. A great deal of work was done on Hadrian's Wall in the time of Severus (AD 193-211) and Caracalla, who must have been very familiar with the whole frontier system, apparently made use of his experience when he came to reconstruct the frontier system in Germany.

on the North Sea to Romania on the Black Sea, although in certain periods it advanced some way beyond this line. The considerable physical barrier formed by the rivers was reinforced by a series of fortifications strung out mostly along the west and south banks. It was presumably felt that the wide rivers made any other continuous barrier (such as a wall) unnecessary.

The frontier in the province of Raetia (roughly modern Switzerland) consisted of a continuous stone wall built by the Emperor Caracalla in the early third century. Caracalla knew Hadrian's Wall well and it would be difficult to believe that the decision to build a stone wall in Raetia was not influenced by what he had seen and experienced in Britain.

There was an even larger frontier to the Empire in Africa, from Mauretania to Tripolitania. The best known section is in the province of Numidia (eastern Algeria and Tunisia), which

The Multangular Tower, York.
This tower marked the western
angle of the legionary fortress at
York. It was one of a series of eight
projecting towers added to the south-
west side of the fortress, probably
around AD 300.

Life-size model of a Roman legionary soldier. The legionaries were heavy infantry, with helmets, body armour, shields, swords, javelins, and much other equipment, all of more or less standard type, unlike the auxiliary troops who tended to use their own native equipment.

Imaginative view of what the Walltown Crags sector of the Wall might have looked like when the frontier system was fully operational (by the late Alan Sorrell).

has the added, considerable interest that it was almost certainly built by Hadrian. The Numidian frontier consisted for most of its length of a stone wall and ditch, further supported by a series of stone towers. These were either single towers or double towers, the latter also providing gateways through the system. There was one double tower every Roman mile and one single tower in between, and this regularity in Hadrian's African frontier is matched by the regularity of the milecastles and turrets on the frontier which he built in the north of England.

There was another extensive frontier on the eastern flank of the Roman Empire, from the Red Sea to the Caspian Sea. One of the better known parts is in Palestine, between the Mediterranean and the Dead Sea, a distance of 75 Roman miles (cf. Hadrian's Wall, 80 Roman miles), where the system consisted of seven forts, thirteen fortlets, eleven watch-towers and four road stations.

The land frontiers of the Roman Empire were of enormous extent: some 3,000 miles in Africa, 2,000 miles in Asia and only marginally less in Europe. The portions described above are quite clearly only small samples of what was obviously a very extensive range of fortifications. Even a cursory survey would involve a separate volume, but hopefully what has been done will enable Hadrian's Wall to be seen in some sort of wider context rather than in complete isolation.

Early Sources of Evidence

There are a number of ancient surviving sources of written information which are important in relation to Hadrian's Wall and will therefore be referred to from time to time throughout the book. The two principal sources are known as the *Notitia Dignitatum* and the Antonine Itinerary. The *Notitia Dignitatum et Administrationum, tam Civilium, tam Militarium, in Partibus Orientis in Partibus Occidentis,* to give it its full title, can be best explained by means of a simple translation: List of offices and duties, both Civil and Military, in the Eastern and Western Parts (of the Empire). As far as Britain is concerned the list relates to the fourth century. Its importance for Hadrian's Wall is that it gives the original Roman names of virtually all the auxiliary forts along the frontier and also the name of the auxiliary units, at least in the period just mentioned.

The Antonine Itinerary (*Itinerarium Provinciarum Antonini Augusti*), is, in effect, a handbook to the road system of the Roman Empire, giving place names along routes with distances between. It dates originally to the time of the Emperor Caracalla, early in the third century. Because two major roads pass through Hadrian's Wall, a number of places in its vicinity are mentioned and have provided valuable evidence in the study of the Wall as a whole.

The Ravenna List or Ravenna Cosmography (*Ravennatis Anonymi Cosmographia*) is of much later date (seventh century), but is apparently based on earlier sources, including (probably) the Antonine Itinerary. It consists of a list of the towns, countries and rivers of the known world, and the British section gives the names, among other places, of the forts along the Wall from east to west.

Two more (limited) sources are the Rudge Cup (found at Rudge, Wiltshire), a small enamelled cup which is inscribed with the names of five forts at the western end of the Wall, and another, similar vessel, known as the Amiens Skillet (found at Amiens, France, in 1949), which names the same five forts plus another one. These five written sources are an important addition to the purely archaeological information, enabling us to fill out the picture with the names of units and the original names of forts. Other sources (inscriptions on gravestones, altars and buildings), give even more detailed information about particular people, the names of commanding officers, centurions and ordinary soldiers, and their families and fortunes.

II
THE WALL
SYSTEM

Hadrian's Wall, by which we mean, as explained earlier, the whole system of defences along the northern frontier of Britain, consisted of: the Wall itself; its associated ditch; the *glacis* or mound on the outer edge of the ditch; the milecastles; the turrets; the auxiliary forts; the Vallum; and the Military Way. These are the features immediately associated with the line of the Wall. In addition, there are the forts, fortlets and towers of the Cumbrian coast which are an extension of the Wall system, and there are also the outpost forts to the north of the Wall which are very much part of the same scheme.

It has been said on more than one occasion that the Wall is by no means always in the best position for observation to the north. Along the high crags in the central sector the outlook to the north is for the most part unrestricted, but even at Housesteads, which is in this sector, the view beyond the immediate foreground is limited, and this is true in a number of other places as well. Why then does the Wall system follow such a line? The answer may, in fact, be very simple. The Wall is where it is because that is where the frontier was when Hadrian decided to build his frontier system. He chose to fortify the line he had already rather than create a new line. In the Stanegate he had a good east-west road for communication, and in the Stanegate forts he had accommodation for most, if not all, of the eventual garrison, although in the event the Stanegate forts were not used, due to a change in plan. Although in the circumstances the best possible line was chosen for the Wall, it was a limited best, restricted to a very narrow strip of territory, just north of the Stanegate. Any wider choice of terrain would have created more problems than it solved. In spite of opportunities presented by extensive rebuilding in later periods the line of the Wall remained virtually unchanged for nearly three centuries, suggesting that the Romans were not unduly perturbed by what may appear to our eyes to be deficiencies in its situation.

Work along the Wall was organized, at one end of the scale, by centuries, each century of 80 men building a length of 45 yards, and marking the two ends of their stretch of Wall with centurial stones, which gave the name of the century responsible for the work. However, there is also evidence, at the other end of the scale, for the organization of the work legion by legion. Although the Wall, milecastles and turrets were built within the terms of a single broad directive, there was quite clearly some room within this for variation, and much of the work of the different legions can be distinguished on this basis. There are, for example, two kinds of milecastle: long axis and short axis. The long axis milecastles have their longer axis at right angles to the Wall, while the short axis ones have their short axis at right angles. Two legions, the Sixth and the Twentieth, appear to have built long-axis

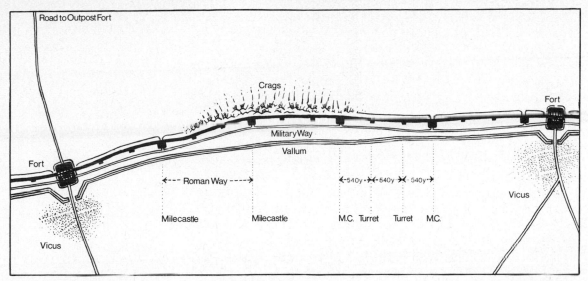

Road to Outpost Fort

Crags

Fort

Military Way

Vallum

Fort

Vicus

←--- Roman Way ---→   ←-540y-→←-540y-→←-540y-→

Milecastle   Milecastle   M.C. Turret   Turret M.C.

Vicus

Hadrian's Wall was, in fact, a whole defence system rather than a simple wall. As completed by Hadrian it consisted (a) of an outer bank of earth, a ditch and the Wall itself; (b) of auxiliary forts (every four or five miles), fortlets or milecastles (every Roman mile), and turrets (at 540 yd. intervals between the milecastles); and (c) of an earthwork known as the Vallum which ran behind, i.e. to the south of, everything mentioned above; the Military Way was a later feature, built probably in the time of Emperor Septimius Severus (AD 193-211). A series of outpost forts to the north and a series down the Cumbrian coast were also built in Hadrian's time.

milecastles and one, the Second, short-axis milecastles. Moreover, the milecastles of the Sixth and Twentieth legions can be further distinguished from each other by the form of their entrance arches. There is a similar variation in the building of the turrets, some having walls 4 feet thick, others walls only 3 feet thick; of the latter some have their doors at the eastern end of the back wall, while others have them at the western end. The different types of milecastles and turrets, and other variations in the Wall itself, make it possible to suggest how the work was organized as far as each legion was concerned, and how it progressed from year to year during the building period.

In a recent book (*Hadrian's Wall*, London, Allen Lane, 1976) David Breeze and Brian Dobson have suggested that work along the Wall was allocated in approximately 5-mile blocks, each legion taking responsibility for one block at a time, building everything within it, Wall, milecastles and turrets. There appear to have been seven legion-sized blocks of work from milecastle 7 to milecastle 49 on the River Irthing, plus a shorter, odd section from milecastle 4 to 7. To the west of the Irthing, where the Wall was originally turf-built, there were another six blocks, from milecastle 40 to turret 80a, at the western terminus of the Wall on Solway Firth. Each of these thirteen sections can be attributed (although only tentatively in some cases) to a particular legion. The biggest omission from this allocation of work are the auxiliary forts, and their inclusion, and that of other features, can be best understood by considering the tentative chronological programme of work put forward by Breeze and Dobson.

Hadrian (they suggest) arrived in Britain in AD 122, accompanied by a new governor, Aulus Platorius Nepos. Probably by the time the decision to build a frontier system was taken it was too late to have a full season's work. There would, in any case, be a great deal of surveying and other preparatory work to be done. They do, however, suggest that the short section from Newcastle westwards (section 4-7, referred to above) was built in this season. The first full season was AD 123. Work appears to have begun at several points simultaneously. At the eastern end part of each legion worked each of three adjacent blocks, 7-12, 12-17, and 17-22. At the same time three adjacent sections were being worked west of the River Irthing (49-54, 54-59a and 59a-64b), in what was then the eastern part of the turf Wall. They also suggest that about half of the 40 miles of Cumbrian coast defences were completed in this year. Thus by the end of the 123 season there would have been some 18 miles of stone Wall, milecastles and turrets (section 4-22), from Newcastle westwards, some 15

Below: In the central sector, from Milecastle 34 westwards to Milecastle 46 the Wall is seen in its most dramatic setting, above the high crags which make an outer ditch superfluous. This is a general view in the Haltwhistle area, near the western end of the high crags sector.

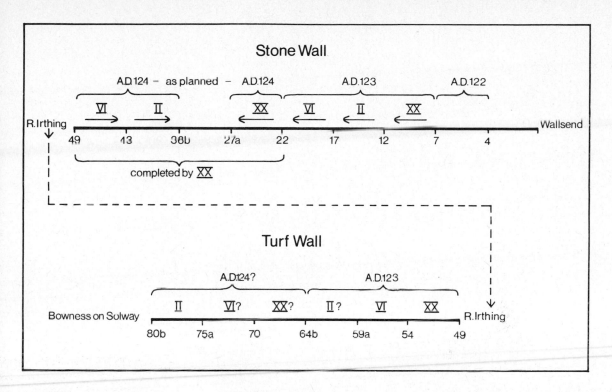

Stone Wall

A.D.124 – as planned – A.D.124   A.D.123   A.D.122

VI   II   XX   VI   II   XX

R.Irthing   Wallsend
49   43   38b   27a   22   17   12   7   4

completed by XX

Turf Wall

A.D.124?   A.D.123

II   VI?   XX?   II?   VI   XX

Bowness on Solway   R.Irthing
80b   75a   70   64b   59a   54   49

Work along the Wall appears to have been organised in five-mile blocks, one legion taking responsibility for everything in that sector, Wall, ditch, glacis, milecastles, turrets and Vallum but not the auxiliary forts which were an addition to the original plan and caused a disruption in the programme of work. The diagram shows the 5 mile blocks, the legions involved, as far as they are known, the year in which the work was done and the direction in which the gangs worked, west to east or east to west.

miles of turf Wall, milecastles and turrets from the Irthing westwards, and about 20 miles of the Cumbrian coast defences.

In the AD 124 season work began on the same lines. It was not, however, completed as planned. There is very clear archaeological evidence, to be detailed later, of a change of plan, and the decision to make this change was probably taken during the AD 124 season. The decision, which radically altered the appearance of the system, was to dispense with the Stanegate forts to the rear and instead to build entirely new auxiliary forts on the Wall itself. This involved not only considerable additional work but also the dismantling of quite a lot of work already done. Gaps wide enough to accommodate auxiliary forts (c 400 feet) had to be made in the Wall, and where the new forts coincided, as they did in a number of cases, with milecastles and turrets, these too had to be dismantled down to their foundations. The result of all this appears to have been a re-allocation of duties to cope with the additional work. There are fourteen forts actually attached to the Wall and one or two others very closely associated with it. This very considerable building job was given to the Second and Sixth legions who were probably kept very fully occupied with it over the next few years. Meanwhile the Twentieth legion was given the task of completing work on the rest of the Wall. The completion of the Cumbrian coast defences, mentioned above, also seems to have been carried out by the Twentieth. By AD 128 the new system was probably substantially complete, Wall, milecastles, turrets, auxiliary forts, etc. Work did in fact, continue after this date but this could well have been on the internal buildings of the forts, the more essential ramparts, gates and ditches no doubt having been completed first.

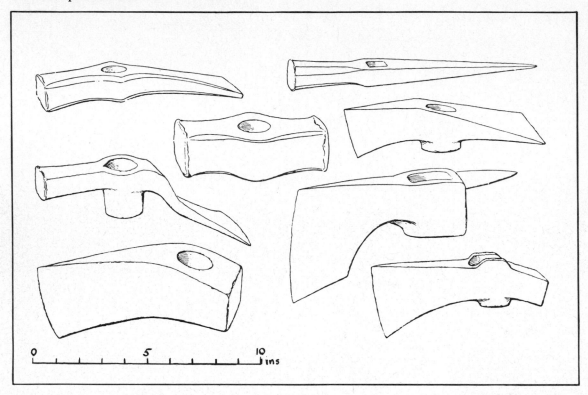

The Wall

As finally completed in stone *c* AD 163, Hadrian's Wall extended for seventy-three miles, from Wallsend in the east to Bowness in the west. However, a substantial part of the Wall was originally turf-built and the sequence of events can be best understood with the aid of the accompanying illustration. In Stage 1 a turf Wall was begun west of the Irthing and a stone Wall, $9\frac{1}{2}$ feet wide, between the river and Newcastle. In Stage 2 the turf Wall was completed as planned but the stone Wall was completed in two parts, one at the planned width of $9\frac{1}{2}$ feet (Broad Wall), and one at a narrower width of $7\frac{1}{2}$ feet (Narrow Wall, on broad foundation). At the same time, the Wall was extended eastwards as far as Wallsend, at $7\frac{1}{2}$ feet width. In Stage 3, about 5 miles of turf Wall was replaced by a stone Wall, $7\frac{1}{2}$ feet wide. Finally, in Stage 4, *c* AD 163, the remaining section of turf Wall was replaced by a stone Wall of intermediate width, $8\frac{1}{2}$ feet. Whatever its width it is generally agreed that the Wall was about 16 feet high to the rampart walk, with another 6 feet for a breastwork, giving an overall

Above: Although the tools illustrated are not specifically associated with the building of the Wall they must be among the types used by the legionary gangs. Other heavy tools would have included picks, mattocks, spades and shovels.

height of about 22 feet. The earlier, turf Wall was somewhat lower and broader with an overall height of around 18 feet including a timber breastwork.

The Ditch

In many places in the central sector the Wall runs above steep crags which render a ditch unnecessary. Apart from this, however, it had in front of it, for the greater part of its length, a standard Roman military ditch, of fairly wide, V-shaped section with a square drainage channel at the bottom. The material excavated from the ditch was placed on its outer, north edge in the form of a wide mound, in military parlance a *glacis* which offered no cover to an attacker while at the same time adding to the effective depth of the ditch.

A portion of the Wall still standing fourteen courses (c.10 ft.) high at Hare Hill.

The building sequence and composition of the Wall: 1. Turf Wall begun and foundations for a (Broad) Stone Wall laid; 2. Turf Wall completed; Stone Wall completed partly as Broad Wall and partly as Narrow Wall on Broad foundation; extension to Wallsend (7½ ft.); 3. Five miles of Turf Wall rebuilt in stone (7½ ft.); 4. Rest of Turf Wall replaced by Stone Wall, (8½ ft.).

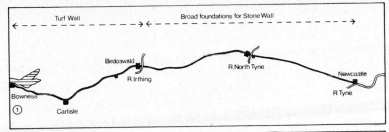

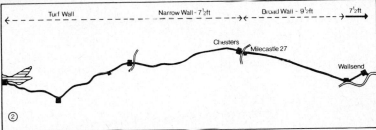

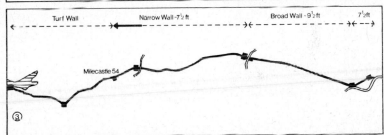

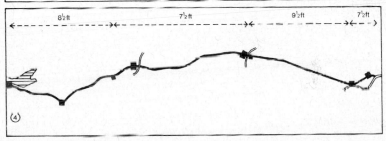

Cross section of the Wall, berm, ditch and glacis. These features formed the continuous linear element in the frontier system, linking together the auxiliary forts, milecastles and turrets. The generally agreed height of the Wall is c.16 ft. to the rampart walk with another 6 ft. or so for the breastwork. The material from the ditch was heaped up to form a broad mound which, in effect widened and deepened the ditch as far as an attacker was concerned.

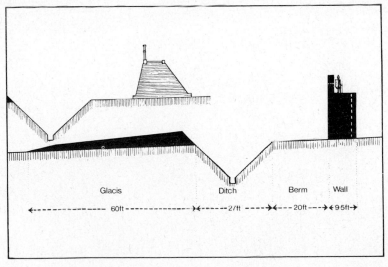

Milecastles

A milecastle is a very small Roman fort, known usually, when free-standing (i.e., not attached to the Wall) as a fortlet, something much smaller than an auxiliary fort. In fact, the fortlets on the Wall are usually around 80 x 90 feet overall, with walls around 8-10 feet thick. There were originally 80 fortlets on Hadrian's Wall, known as milecastles because of their regular spacing every Roman mile (1,620 yards). Two of these were eliminated when the auxiliary forts were added to the Wall system. Milecastle 43 now lies beneath Great Chesters fort, and milecastle 80 beneath the fort at Bowness. Each milecastle was large enough to house 50 or 60 men, although the complement was often much less than this. Smaller garrisons may have become possible when the overall tactics of the Wall were changed. The milecastles in the original turf-built sector of the Wall were also turf-built. When the turf Wall was replaced by a stone Wall, the milecastles were likewise replaced by stone milecastles.

There are good examples of milecastles at Cawfields (M.C. 42), Poltross Burn (M.C. 48), Housesteads (M.C. 37), and Harrow's Scar (M.C. 49). The two latter will be dealt with in Chapters IV and VI respectively. Cawfields is a short-axis

Reconstruction drawing of a stone-built milecastle. There were originally eighty milecastles, one every Roman mile, along the length of Hadrian's Wall.

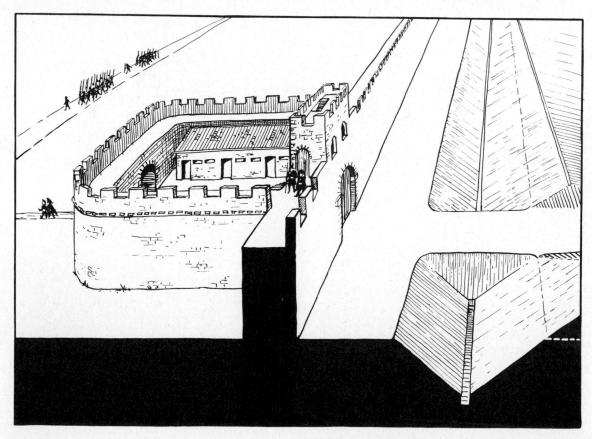

Below: The legions involved in the building of the Wall built milecastles to slightly different plans although always within the terms of a single overall directive. Two legions (VI, XX) built long-axis milecastles, i.e. the longer axis was *a right angle to the Wall (a), while the third legion (II) built the short axis variety, with the short axis at right angles to the Wall (b).* *Bottom: Comparative plans of turf-built and stone-built milecastles. Although they look rather different in overall area, this is due almost entirely to the much greater thickness of the turf ramparts. Internally the space available is virtually the same.*

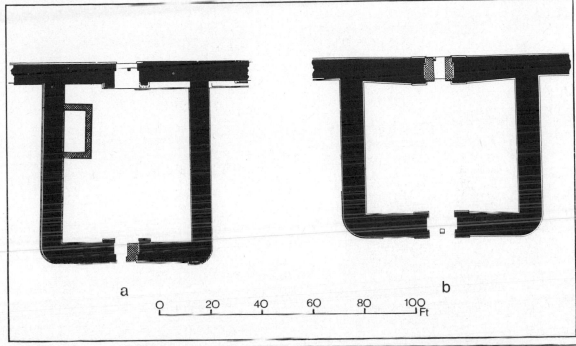

a   b

0   20   40   60   80   100 Ft.

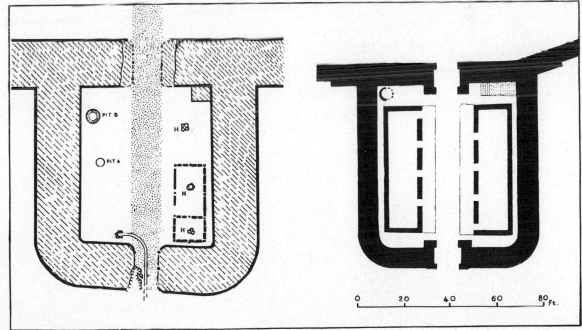

0   20   40   60   80 Ft.

milecastle. The most noticeable feature is the way in which the ground on which it stands slopes down away from the Wall, so that the interior space could not have been very convenient. The same inconvenience can be seen at Poltress Burn (long axis) where the ground slopes upwards from the Wall. A slight shift of position would have produced a level interior, but presumably orders were rigidly obeyed as to spacing and Poltross Burn milecastle was built where exact measurement indicated. For convenience, milecastles are numbered from east to west, including the two eliminated by later forts, so that Milecastle 1 is just to the west of Wallsend fort and Milecastle 80 is under the last fort at the western end of the Wall, Bowness.

Reconstruction drawing of a turf-built milecastle. In the western sector, west of the River Irthing, the milecastles, like the Wall itself, were originally built of turf and timber. When the Wall was rebuilt in stone, so too were the milecastles.

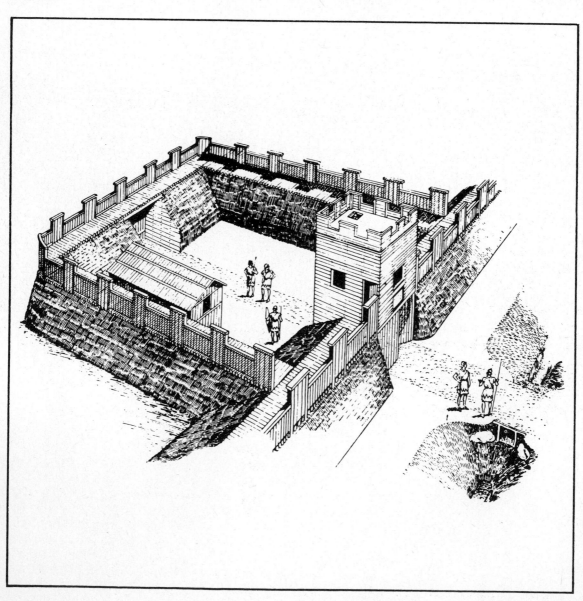

Turrets

The milecastle at Poltross Burn, with remains of the internal buildings. This too is easily accessible, a few minutes walk from a car park in Gilsland village, on the B6318, about two miles west of Greenhead.

The same numbering system is used to identify the turrets or towers along the Wall. There are two of these between each milecastle at intervals of 540 yards and they are numbered according to the number of the milecastle immediately to the east, and further distinguished by the letters a and b. Thus, the first turret to the west of, say, Milecastle 43, is turret 43a and the second turret 43b and so on along the whole Wall. Turrets are simply square towers about 14 x 14 ft inside and 20 x 20 ft externally, built into the structure of the Wall so that only half of their area projected to the rear. Unlike the milecastles the turrets in the turf Wall section were built from the start in stone. When the turf Wall was rebuilt in stone they were simply incorporated in it ready-built. The turrets probably rose at least one storey above the general level of the Wall.

Opposite: The remains of the turret at Limestone corner, about two miles west of Chesters fort on the B6318.

Below: Plans and elevations of the Wall turrets.

Bottom: Both turrets and milecastles were built with short sections of Broad Wall on either side ready to bond into the Wall when it was built. Where the Wall actually was built a Narrow Wall than there is now a noticeable step-back in the thickness of the Wall, about twelve feet on either side of the turret or milecastle involved.

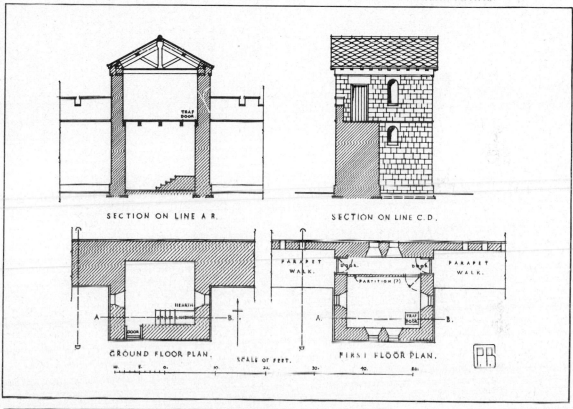

SECTION ON LINE A B.

SECTION ON LINE C.D.

GROUND FLOOR PLAN.

SCALE OF FEET.

FIRST FLOOR PLAN.

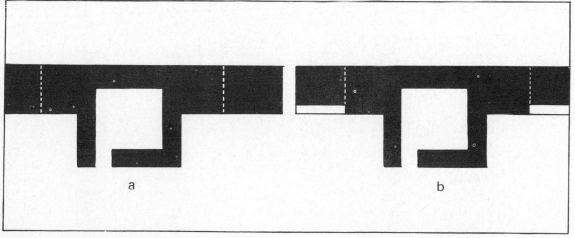

a

b

The Stanegate Forts

The Wall, milecastles and turrets represent the scheme as originally conceived. The main body of troops was to be housed in a line of forts to the rear, along the Stanegate, the road from Corbridge to Carlisle, although additional forts would have been required at the eastern and western ends. Some of the Stanegate forts were built forty years earlier by Agricola, among them Corbridge, Vindolanda, Nether Denton and Carlisle. To supplement these new forts were built at Newbrough, Haltwhistle Burn, Throp, Boothby, Brampton Old Church, and High Crosby. While the Wall was still being built it was decided to put the forts housing the main garrison on the Wall itself. The Stanegate forts were dismantled, although Corbridge and Vindolanda were retained and remained in use throughout most of the Roman occupation.

Map of the auxiliary forts along Hadrian's Wall. These were not, in fact, part of the system as first conceived. Originally there were to be only milecastles and turrets along the Wall, the main garrison being housed to the rear in a series of forts along the Stanegate. However, even while the system was being built there was a change of plan and the forts were placed on the Wall itself, sections of the Wall, and occasionally turrets and milecastles, being removed to make way for the additional structures.

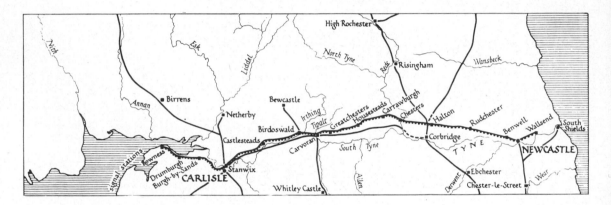

The Wall Forts

There are fourteen forts actually attached to the Wall and one, Castlesteads, about 400 yards to the rear but quite clearly included in the Wall system by the Vallum, which swings away from its normal line to take it in. The other fourteen forts are, from east to west: Wallsend, Newcastle, Benwell, Rudchester, Halton Chesters, Chesters, Carrawbrough, Housesteads, Great Chesters, Birdoswald (Castlesteads between) Stanwix, Burgh-by-Sands, Drumburgh and Bowness. Another fort, Carvoran, is very close to the Wall (between Great Chesters and Birdoswald), but is excluded by the Vallum, and its connection would appear to be with the Stanegate where it guarded the road junction with the Maiden Way.

The gaps between the forts vary considerably, from about two miles, between Newcastle and Benwell, to about seven miles between Birdoswald and Castlesteads. The average distance is just under five miles. The fourteen attached forts can be divided into groups, according to the way in which they are related to the Wall. Six forts straddle the Wall—i.e., they project beyond it to the north as well as to the south. Seven others are flush with the Wall—i.e., the Wall forms their north side and they project only to the south. In one case, Newcastle, the site is almost completely obscured by the city buildings and its exact relationship to the Wall is unknown. At Birdoswald both relationships were involved. As built it projected to the north, beyond the turf Wall. However, when the latter was replaced, the stone Wall took a different line and ran up to the north corners of the fort, making it of the flush variety. The projecting forts are mostly in the eastern sector of the Wall, at Wallsend, Benwell, Rudchester, Halton and Chesters. Beyond Chesters to the west, Carrawbrough, Housesteads, Great Chesters, Birdoswald (originally projecting), Stanwix, Drumburgh and Bowness are flush with the Wall. The exception in this western sector is Burgh-by-Sands which, like the eastern forts, projected to the north of the Wall.

The projecting forts are presumed to have been intended for cavalry units and those flush with the Wall for infantry units, although this view has been questioned recently. The projecting forts have no less than three of their main gateways opening to the north of the Wall. Far from being defensive structures they are quite clearly designed to allow very rapid movement out of the forts to the north, to engage the enemy in the open where the Roman army was at its best. Whatever type of unit they were intended for, cavalry or infantry, or a

The auxiliary forts are linked to the Wall in two ways. Either they are flush with it, so that their northern ramparts are in line with the Wall, or they straddle it, so that about a third of the fort projects beyond the Wall to the north, together with three of the four principal entrances.

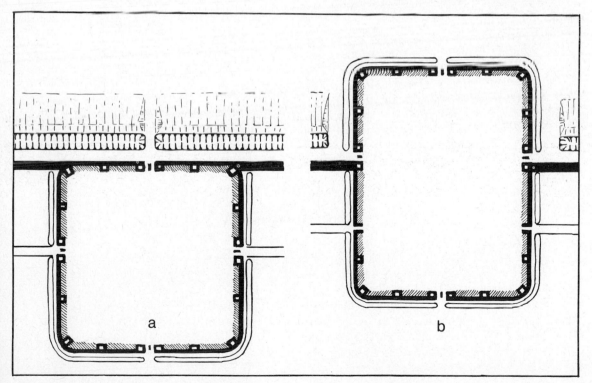

a   b

mixture of the two, the existence of three gates north of the Wall would have allowed for more rapid deployment of forces than one, and it may have been speed rather than anything else which dictated the projecting design.

The Vallum

At varying distances behind the Wall and its associated features, but usually quite close, within a couple of hundred feet, is a feature called the Vallum. The word Vallum actually means rampart in Latin and presumably arose because it was considered that the features involved were defensive in character. The central feature of the Vallum was, in fact, a ditch, with the material excavated from it piled in two carefully-built mounds set 30 feet back from each edge. The overall width of the whole structure was 120 feet, the Roman Surveyor's unit of length called an *actus*. If it was a defensive feature it was quite unlike any normal Roman military work and, in fact, quite unsuitable for defensive purposes.

The approach road to each fort from the south passed through the Vallum by means of gaps in the north and south mounds and by a corresponding causeway across the central ditch, where the most important feature was a gateway, which was apparently controlled from the north—i.e., from the fort. There were similar gates at the milecastles, but there was no corresponding gap in the south mound. In other words, these gates were meant to provide access for the milecastle garrison to the Vallum area. They did not permit direct access to the milecastles from the south.

The purpose of the Vallum has been the subject of a great deal of controversy, particularly in the early days of research on the Wall. Among the suggestions were that this was, in fact, Hadrian's frontier, the Wall, milecastles, turrets etc. in front being the work of the later Emperor Septimius Severus (AD 193-211). Another suggestion was that the Vallum was a customs barrier and that the gates across the causeway were

Cross-section of the Vallum, the earthwork to the rear of the main defence system. This was quite clearly not a defensive work and was probably intended as a very clear and unmistakable boundary, marking off military zone immediately behind the Wall.

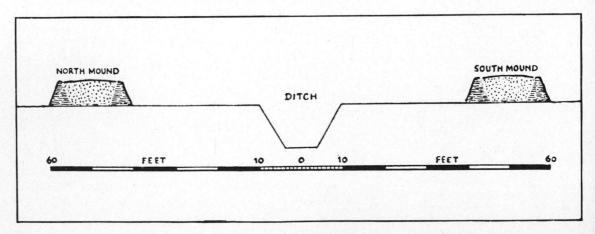

manned by customs officers, although this could not apply to the gates at the milecastles since there is no gap in the south mound. However, these give the clue to the probable function of the Vallum. They allow access to the Vallum area, but only from the milecastles, not from the area to the south. In other words, the Vallum marks off a military zone immediately behind the Wall which is not accessible to the civilian population. The gateways at the forts tell the same story. They were not fortified gateways, but they were effective barriers across the road leading to the forts through which the military could pass, but which were closed at other times to prevent civilian access. The Vallum also provided a closed zone along which the Wall garrison could carry out patrol work and normal military movements without hindrance from civilian traffic.

The Military Way

As first completed east-west communication was by means of the Stanegate and thence by branch roads north to each fort. Only at a later stage, possibly associated with rebuilding work on the Wall under Septimius Severus in the years AD 198-208, was there a purpose-built road, generally called the Military Way, much more closely associated with the Wall and much more closely geared to its needs. It was a normal Roman road, some twenty feet wide with a base and kerbs of heavy stone, a core of small stone and a top surface, heavily cambered, of fine gravel. By the time the road was built the Vallum had gone out of use since in places the road runs along the top of the north mound. The Military Way ran close to the Wall in most places. Where the terrain was difficult the road often swung away from the Wall to find the easiest approach to the milecastles and forts, and a great deal of ingenuity was displayed by the road engineers.

The Cumbrian Coast Defences

In all linear defence systems such as Hadrian's Wall one of the greatest dangers is that of being by-passed, and there was a real danger of this at the western end of Hadrian's Wall. Beyond Bowness, the Cumbrian coast looks across Solway Firth towards south-west Scotland, always a potential source of trouble for the Romans. That the Romans recognised this danger immediately is clear from the fact that the Cumbrian coast defences were an integral part of the original plan. The major difference was in the absence of the Wall, and in this respect the Cumbrian coast was treated in the same way as the Roman frontier in Europe along the Rhine and the Danube where the rivers provided the continuous linear element in the system.

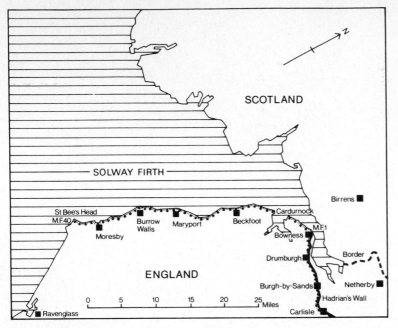

Although the Wall itself stopped at Bowness on Solway, Hadrian's system of defences continued down the Cumbrian coast for another forty miles. It consisted of fortlets every Roman mile with two towers between each, exactly as between Bowness and Wallsend except for the linking Wall. When the auxiliary forts were added to the Wall they were added also to the Cumbrian coast system, four of them being inserted into the line of defences at Beckfoot, Maryport, Burrow Walls and Moresby.

The Cumbrian coast system consisted originally of milefortlets (thus called to distinguish them from the milecastles attached to the Wall), and towers (to distinguish them from the Wall turrets). Both types were, of course, now free-standing, but they were spaced out in exactly the same way as the milecastles and turrets along the Wall and similarly numbered, starting with milefortlet No 1 (Biglands), just one Roman mile along the coast to the west of Bowness, and continuing as far as St Bees Head where milefortlet 40 would have been located. While the towers, like the turrets on the Wall, were always of stone, some of the milefortlets were turf-built, and seem never to have been rebuilt in stone.

One of the most interesting developments of recent years has been the discovery, by Professor G D B Jones of Manchester University, of additional features in the Cumbrian coast system, in the area between Bowness and Cardurnock. These consist of parallel ditches about 135 feet apart, between which the milefortlets and towers are placed. The ditches are quite small, only about 6 feet wide and a couple of feet deep, and appear to have had timber fences or palisades on their outer edges. This would not have presented much of an obstacle to an enemy and the structure cannot be seen in terms of defence. It probably marks off a military zone between the milefortlets and towers not to be trespassed on, and to an enemy it was a clear and unmistakable mark on the ground that this was the frontier of the Roman Empire. It was probably more of a psychological and moral barrier than a military one, not only to the enemy in front but also to the inhabitants of Cumbria behind.

The auxiliary forts in the Cumbrian coast sector seem to have been added to the milefortlets and towers in the same way as they were added along the Wall, and presumably at the same time, as a result of the same change of plan. There are four forts involved, Beckfoot, Maryport, Burrow Walls and Moresby.

The Outpost Forts to the North

A series of forts to the north of the Wall are generally included under the heading of outposts, and can be divided into two groups, east and west. The western group consists of three sites: Bewcastle, Netherby and Birrens. Bewcastle, about 7 miles beyond Birdoswald, was linked to it by road. Another road linked the Wall fort at Carlisle (Stanwix) to Netherby, and from there another road ran west to Birrens. These forts were built at the same time as the rest of the frontier system and were probably completed by c AD 130. The traditional view has been that they were designed to make good deficiencies in the outlook to the north which is not as good as in the central and eastern sectors of the Wall. This may well be so, although Breeze and Dobson have recently suggested that the three forts were intended to guard, and no doubt control, a portion of Brigantian territory which was left beyond the Wall when the frontier system was built. In fact, the two functions are not so very different and both may have formed part of Roman thinking when the sites were planned. By their very existence they protected the area in which they stood, and by their position they gave early warning of trouble north of the Wall. Which consideration, if either, predominated in the Roman mind is a matter for speculation.

A series of forts to the north of the Wall formed a system of outposts, some of which were part of Hadrian's original plan. The three western outpost forts, Bewcastle, Netherby and Birrens were built at the same time as the main Wall system and were clearly intended to be integral parts of the whole scheme of defence. The five eastern outposts appear to have been added towards the end of the second century and, together with the three existing forts, formed a deep zone in front of the Wall which was regularly patrolled so that early warning could be given of hostile movement as much as thirty or forty miles away.

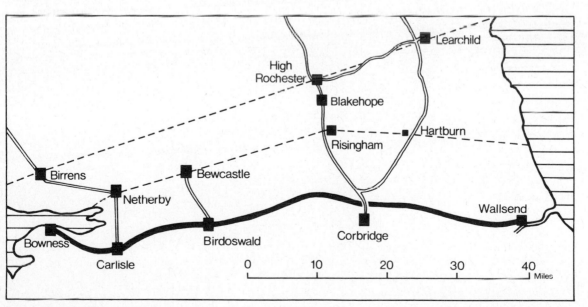

The eastern group of outpost forts consists of five sites, although not all of them remained in use for the whole period of the Wall's history. They are Risingham, Blakehope, High Rochester, Learchild and Hartburn, the latter a fortlet rather than a full-scale fort. These eastern outpost forts do not appear to have been part of the original scheme but to have been added later. They are usually attributed to the period of the Emperor Septimius Severus, early in the third century, but they could be earlier and a date of *c* AD 170 has been suggested—i.e., following the re-occupation of Hadrian's Wall in *c* AD 163.

Between them the eastern and western outpost forts, eight in all, define a zone in front of the Wall from fifteen (in the west) to thirty miles deep (in the east). The outer edge of this zone is formed by Birrens, High Rochester and Learchild which are virtually in a straight line, some 60 miles long. At a later stage, possibly during the third century, the outer forts seem to have been given up, narrowing the zone to a depth of about ten miles, based on Netherby, Bewcastle, Risingham and Hartburn. The possible functions of these zones in relation to the Wall are among the matters to be considered in the next section, the tactical use of Hadrian's Wall by the Romans.

The Tactics of Hadrian's Wall

The thickness and (presumed) height of the Wall almost inevitably make one think of it in defensive terms, of Roman soldiers fighting valiantly from the rampart walk against the massed tribesmen below and eventually driving them away, to leave the Empire's most northerly frontier still intact and the province unmolested. Such a picture would, however, be very misleading. Although there may have been occasions during the three centuries when engagements were fought in this way, they must have been the exception rather than the rule. The Wall was not designed for such use and these tactics were, in any case, contrary to normal Roman military practice. The Romans would never wait passively behind defences for an enemy to attack them. They would always choose to meet him in the open where the Roman army was at its best, and where its discipline, organization and training could be used to full effect. In static, defensive positions these qualities were largely wasted.

The Wall itself was not so much a fighting platform as, among other things, an elevated patrol track. It would certainly have stopped the movement of individuals and small groups across the frontier, but by itself it would never have stopped an army, even a native one, nor was it intended to do so. There simply would not have been sufficient room on top of the Wall for the number of Roman soldiers required for such a task. As much as anything else the Wall was an unmistakable mark on the ground that here was the frontier of Roman Britain; to attack this was to attack the mighty Roman Empire and risk retribution on fearful scale. Rather than a line to be defended from behind, the Wall was a springboard for attack, or counter attack, against any enemy who showed signs of aggressive intent against the province of Britannia.

The structure of the system tells the same story. The numerous gateways through the Wall (at every milecastle, with one, and sometimes three, double gateways at the forts) are not indicative of a defensive attitude. If the Wall had been intended simply as a barrier then it would have been provided with as few gates as possible. Instead it had well over one hundred gates, and these can only have been for Roman purposes, to facilitate the tactics for which the Wall was designed. With so many exits the Romans could deploy their forces with great speed and meet and dispose of any threat in the open, where they were at their best, long before an enemy could do any harm. At the approach of an enemy force the Romans could move men along behind the Wall, under complete cover, to emerge from a series of gates, either simultaneously or according to some other pre-arranged plan, leaving the enemy surprised and confused and not knowing what to expect next. Pincerlike movements could cut off any retreat and pin him against the very barrier he was trying to attack.

These are generally presumed to be the Hadrianic tactics, associated with the design of the Wall as completed c AD 128, in which the enemy was dealt with fairly close to the Wall. Later in the century, or possibly early in the following century, there seems to have been a change in tactics, associated with the outpost forts mentioned earlier and the deep zone in front of the Wall which they covered. The new tactics seem to have been to hold not only the Wall but also a deep zone in front of it, protected by the forts mentioned earlier and regularly patrolled, so that any movement into it could be detected at an early stage and dealt with long before it reached the

Hadrian's Wall seems to have been designed originally to deal with the enemy fairly close to the Wall, using it as a screen to conceal the movement of troops, and the milecastle gateways as sally ports from which to emerge and take the enemy by surprise. At a later stage, from c.AD 200 on, the outpost forts and the regular patrols formed an early warning system which allowed the enemy to be dealt with long before he came anywhere near the Wall. As a result many of the milecastles went out of use in this period, their gateways through the Wall being blocked up.

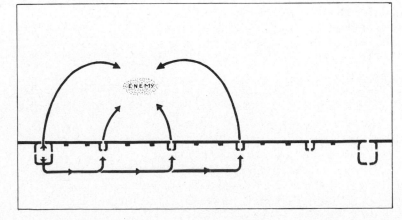

frontier. In the case of a very serious threat the depth of the zone and the early warning which it allowed enabled the Romans to deploy forces from a number of forts to best advantage. The space also allowed them much more scope in methods of dealing with the attack. Such a system, of course, reduced the importance of the milecastles since you cannot surprise an enemy over a distance of several miles. The consequence was that during reconstruction around the turn of the century (c AD 200) many of the milecastle gates through the Wall were reduced in width from around 10 feet to a mere three or four feet. The reduction can be seen very clearly in milecastle 37 just west of Housesteads fort. At or around the same time many of the turrets seem to have gone out of use, and this, together with the treatment of the milecastles, suggests that patrolling along the Wall was no longer considered necessary. This is understandable under the new system. In effect, the patrolling had been moved forward into the zone in front of the Wall, defined by the eight outpost forts, and the intensive patrolling of the Wall itself was no longer necessary. The deep zone (15-30 miles deep), defined by Birrens, High Rochester and Learchild was later reduced to one about ten miles deep and, as far as is known at present, the forts defining this narrower zone, and the zone itself, remained in operation until the latter part of the fourth century.

III

THE HISTORY OF THE WALL

DEO
MARTI
BRACIACÆ
OS TIVS
CAECILIANS
PRAEFCOH
IAQVITANO
V   S

In spite of being in a remote province, on the outer fringes of the Empire, Hadrian's Wall was, on more than one occasion, bound up with events at the centre of power in Rome, at least in those periods when we have any knowledge of its history. There are, in fact, long periods when nothing is recorded about Hadrian's Wall and it is generally presumed that in these periods the Wall was doing the job for which it was designed and that therefore nothing worth recording was happening. When historical record does bring the Wall to our attention then it is often in dramatic circumstances, and not infrequently these circumstances are closely linked to what was happening in Rome and the Roman Empire at large. The fact that Britain needed a strong garrison—i.e., that it had a permanent and substantial army of legionaries and auxiliary troops, had not a little to do with its involvement in the larger politics of the Roman Empire and the struggles for Imperial power which became more frequent as time went on, particularly in the third and fourth centuries AD.

The defence system which we call Hadrian's Wall was substantially complete by c AD 128-130. Despite the enormous effort that had gone into construction, however, it remained as the frontier for only about ten or eleven years, at least in its first phase. Hadrian died in AD 138 and very shortly afterwards his successor as Emperor, Antoninus Pius, through the Governor of Britain, Lollius Urbicus, began preparations for an advance beyond the Wall into Lowland Scotland. The first moves in this undertaking were made in AD 139 and by AD 142 or 143 a new frontier, the Antonine Wall, was established some eighty miles to the north-west, on the Clyde-Forth line, used half a century before by Agricola.

The Antonine Wall

Unlike Hadrian's Wall the Antonine Wall was turf-built throughout and was never rebuilt in stone. It was narrower than the turf-built section of Hadrian's Wall, only 14 feet wide as compared with 20 feet, but it was built on a stone foundation. The sides sloped inwards at an angle of about 70 degrees. It was probably about 10 feet high with a timber rampart walk and a timber breastwork about 6 feet high on the outer edge. In front of the turf rampart was a ditch, separated by a berm or space from 20-40 feet wide, but occasionally wider. The ditch was normally c 40 feet wide and 12 feet deep with a square drainage channel at the bottom. The material excavated from it was placed on its outer edge in the form of a glacis in the same way as on Hadrian's Wall. From east to west the whole wall was only some 36 miles long, just half the length of the Wall it replaced.

In spite of its shorter length there were more forts on the Antonine Wall, nineteen in all, an average of one every two miles, as compared with one every five miles on Hadrian's Wall. These Antonine forts were quite clearly part of the original plan and not a later addition. In fact, the sequence of work seems to indicate that, if anything, the forts were built first, and were then linked by the turf wall. The forts, with two exceptions, were turf-built, although the headquarters and granaries seem to have been of stone, with barracks and other buildings of timber. The two exceptions are Castlecary and Balmuidy which had stone ramparts, probably because there was plenty of stone available in the locality. The forts were usually surrounded by two or three defensive ditches. The *vici* or civil settlements attached to some of them were located in annexes defended in the same way as the forts. The *vici* along Hadrian's Wall were undefended settlements.

It has usually been assumed that the close spacing of the forts along the Antonine Wall made any intermediate features (such as milecastles or turrets) unnecessary. However, there are indications, from excavation and aerial photographic surveys, of smaller structures which appear to be similar to milecastles. If these were a regular feature then there would have been one or two between each fort as part of the completed scheme. There may also have been turrets or towers, but these, if timber built, would be very difficult to detect in the remains of a turf wall. It has also been suggested that some of the earlier Agricolan forts were used in the new line, and claims of up to half the total have been made. Although this number is not now generally accepted, it seems unlikely that the earlier Agricolan forts were completely ignored or discounted in making the new defence line. One or two at least must have their origins in Agricolan structures.

What were the reasons for this early abandonment of Hadrian's very elaborate and very expensive frontier? One reason would seem to have been disturbances among the tribes immediately beyond the Wall. They must have bitterly resented the construction of Hadrian's Wall which very effectively curtailed their raiding and plundering activities into the richer, Roman parts of Britain. The creation of a physical barrier from sea to sea meant that it was no longer possible for them to infiltrate the province, take advantage of their more law-abiding neighbours and slip out again with their gains without being apprehended. In the decade after the Wall's completion these tribes had been a constant source of trouble and it may have been, among other reasons, to find a final solution to this problem that the decision was taken to extend Roman power and control beyond Hadrian's Wall. It may also have been felt that the Antonine Wall, because it was shorter, would be more economical in terms of manpower. There is also a real possibility that the original intention was to do what Agricola had attempted to do some sixty years before, to conquer Scotland using the new wall as the springboard,

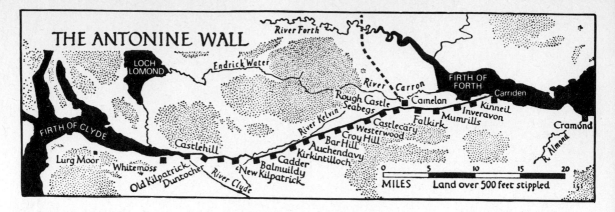

THE ANTONINE WALL

River Forth
LOCH LOMOND
Endrick Water
River Carron
FIRTH OF FORTH
Carriden
FIRTH OF CLYDE
Rough Castle
Seabegs
Camelon
Kinneil
Inveravon
Mumrills
River Kelvin
Castlecary
Westerwood
Croy Hill
Bar Hill
Falkirk
Cramond
Castlehill
Auchendavy
Kirkintilloch
Cadder
Lurg Moor
Whitemoss
Balmuildy
Old Kilpatrick
Duntocher
New Kilpatrick
River Clyde
0   5   10   15   20
MILES   Land over 500 feet stippled

thus extending the province to take in the whole of Britain. When this became impossible to achieve, then the frontier settled on the Antonine Wall, a result of necessity rather than an original objective. Even with this line the Emperor could claim an expansion of Roman territory and some degree of prestige.

The move forward to the Antonine Wall, even if Hadrian's Wall was still held with a skeleton force, removed much of the restraint on the Brigantes in the north of England. They had been quiet for so long that the Romans may have been tempted to believe that they would cause no further trouble. There was indeed no immediate trouble and in the intervening period (i.e., from *c* AD 142-155) the status of Hadrian's Wall was reduced by the provision of numerous ways through the Vallum and by the removal of gates in the milecastles, to provide unimpeded movement to all and sundry across the former frontier and its defences. The real frontier was now eighty miles to the north and Hadrian's Wall and its appurtenances were simply interesting remnants still visible on the ground.

In AD 155, however, the Brigantes of northern England proved once again that they could not be taken for granted. There was an uprising, on how big a scale it is difficult to say, but certainly sufficiently large to have caused, at least temporarily, a withdrawal, after some thirteen years of use, from the Antonine Wall. Eventually the revolt was quelled and the Antonine Wall re-occupied. At a later stage it was abandoned again, this time for good, and Hadrian's Wall became the frontier once again. The dates for this sequence of events have been the cause of much speculation and discussion, most recently by Drs. Breeze and Dobson (1976).

As they point out, what must be fitted into the period between AD 140 and AD 200 are two occupations of the Antonine Wall, with only a short interval between, and two re-occupations of Hadrian's Wall. The sequence of events starts with the Brigantian revolt of AD 155, which may, among other things, have led to the abandonment of the plans to conquer

The Antonine Wall, which was turf built throughout, as were most of its forts, was much shorter than Hadrian's Wall, only about thirty-six miles long, as compared with seventy-three. Its forts, however, were much more closely-spaced than the earlier line, one every two miles as compared with one every five miles for Hadrian's Wall.

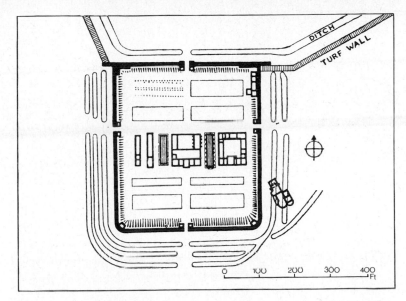

Only two forts on the Antonine Wall were stone-built, Castlecary and the one illustrated above, Balmuidy. The Antonine forts were built before the wall itself, and the two wing walls for bonding into the turf wall are clearly visible in the plan.

the whole of Scotland. Troops would have been pulled back to deal with the trouble and one of the obvious ways of doing this would have been to make use of the former frontier defences on the edge of Brigantian territory. There is evidence of rebuilding on Hadrian's Wall in AD 158, so that between 155 and 158 (possibly in AD 156) it looks as if the Antonine Wall was abandoned (ending its first occupation) and Hadrian's Wall was re-occupied (first re-occupation). The evidence from the Antonine Wall is of a very orderly, strategic withdrawal, with the troops destroying everything they left behind.

The next event to be fitted into the sequence is the occupation of the Antonine Wall for the second time. Now the archaeological evidence indicates only a very short break between the two Antonine occupations, perhaps only a year or two, so that possibly by *c* AD 160 the frontier was back in Scotland once again. However, shortly after this again there is evidence of considerable building work along Hadrian's Wall, *c* AD 163 and later, and the pottery evidence also indicates that the Antonine Wall was finally abandoned in the early sixties, leading to the second re-occupation of Hadrian's Wall. This is a much more compact sequence in time than has been suggested in the past where the second re-occupation of Hadrian's Wall has sometimes been dated nearer the end of the century, *c* AD 180-200, and, of course, this compact sequence still needs final proof.

The question which does arise, if this sequence is correct, is why there was such a rapid series of changes which must have been very wasteful of effort and resources. Although the first change, the withdrawal from the Antonine Wall *c* 155-6, was probably a military necessity, the subsequent changes cannot be justified in this way. Breeze and Dobson suggest that these later decisions were made not in Britain, but in Rome, and were closely bound up with Imperial prestige and the larger policies of the Empire. Hadrian's policy was that of stabilizing frontiers after centuries of steady Roman expansion, and the construction of Hadrian's Wall was very much part of that policy. His successor, Antoninus Pius, reverted to the earlier policy, and although the whole of Scotland was not conquered he at least had the Lowland area to show for his efforts. When that was given up during the Brigantian revolt he saw one of his claims to Imperial prestige disappearing. He therefore, it is suggested, ordered the re-occupation of Lowland Scotland and of the Antonine Wall. With the Brigantian trouble presumably settled this was done and by, perhaps, AD 159 or 160 the frontier was once more on the Tyne-Forth line.

This accounts for the two occupations of the Antonine Wall and for one re-occupation of Hadrian's Wall, but not yet the second. Shortly after the (presumed) re-occupation of the Antonine Wall, Antoninus Pius died, in AD 161. The new Emperor was Marcus Aurelius, and there is historical evidence of trouble in Britain early in his reign which may have impelled him to return to Hadrian's frontier. Certainly there is evidence in the form of building inscriptions for work on some of the Wall forts during the sixties, for whatever reasons, and this confirms that during this period the frontier was formed by Hadrian's Wall. If the hypothesis just outlined is correct, then this is where the frontier remained for the next 250 years, during the remainder of the Roman occupation. In the absence of conclusive proof this is as good as, if not indeed better than, most of the existing hypotheses on the relationship between Hadrian's Wall and the Antonine Wall, and for working purposes will be accepted here, at least provisionally.

In AD 180 the Emperor Marcus Aurelius died, the last of what are generally regarded as the 'good emperors' (Nerva, Trajan, Hadrian, Antoninus Pius), who occupied the greater part of the second century. Unfortunately, Marcus Aurelius was not blessed with a son capable of sustaining the high tradition that had gone before. Commodus lacked the sterling qualities of his predecessors and his accession marked the beginning of the progressive decline in the fortunes of the Roman Empire, although there were still, from time to time, a few men worthy of the high office they occupied.

There were troubles for Britain almost as soon as the reign of Commodus began, including a serious uprising among the Scottish tribes (AD 181), which resulted in the death of a Roman general and the loss of a considerable number of troops. There is recorded evidence that the insurgent tribes crossed the 'Wall', but which 'Wall' is not stated, although in view of what has just been said it must now be assumed that it was Hadrian's Wall. Commodus sent Ulpius Marcellus to deal with the situation, but even so the resultant war lasted six years (until AD 187). It looks as if there was a break through the Wall

Between Birdoswald fort and Harrow's Scar milecastle, about a quarter of a mile to the east, is a very well-preserved section of Wall still standing up to 8 ft. high.

The remains of the milecastle at Cawfields. This is easily accessible from a car park a few minutes walk away, reached by a side road from the B6318 at Haltwhistle Burn.

The Vallum at Limestone Corner, about two miles west of Chesters. Although it formed part of Hadrian's original scheme the Vallum remained in use for only a generation or two, as compared with nearly three centuries for the rest of the Wall.

General view of the Housesteads area.

The Vallum at Sewingshields, about two miles east of Housesteads.

Opposite: The north granary at Housesteads. The granary floor was supported by rows of short piers, about two feet high, which allowed air to circulate freely beneath with the aim of keeping the stored grain fresh and dry.

during this affair. There is evidence of re-building at Halton Chesters, Rudchester and Corbridge, which are all close together, so that the breach was probably a localized one and not the wholesale overwhelming which is so often adduced to explain events along the Wall (below). There appears to be no evidence of re-building at other sites at this time. However, the work of Marcellus at the three sites mentioned may have been the beginning of a programme of renovating all the forts along the Wall during the next forty years or so. This work is generally attributed to the Emperor Septimius Severus and the period AD 198-208, following the events of AD 197, but this view has been questioned recently.

The Emperor Commodus was assassinated in AD 192. At the time the governor of Britain was Clodius Albinus, a wealthy and ambitious man, an able soldier and a very popular figure with the army. The army had made Emperors before and, with no obvious successor to Commodus, it must have occurred to Albinus that here was a golden opportunity for Imperial power if he wished to seize it. Events in Rome must have helped him to make up his mind. After the death of Pertinax, himself formerly a governor of Britain and Emperor for about three months, the Imperial Guard actually put the office of Emperor up for auction to the highest bidder, and news of this disgraceful procedure impelled the army of Britain to proclaim their own popular candidate, Clodius Albinus, as Emperor, in AD 193. Incidentally, the highest bidder at the auction was Didius Julianus, but he, like Pertinax before him, lasted only a matter of months and was dead before the middle of the year, killed by order of the Senate on the arrival in Rome of another, and eventually successful, contender for Imperial power, Septimius Severus.

The sequence of events in Rome (the death of Commodus, then of Pertinax, and then the auction), had its effects not only in Britain but in other parts of the Empire as well. Like Britain, other frontier provinces required substantial armies and the commanders of such forces were in a very strong position when it came to contests for Imperial power. On the Syrian frontier Pescennius Niger, and on the Danube frontier Septimius Severus, were both proclaimed Emperor in addition to Clodius Albinus, and it was soon clear that whoever wished to be Emperor would have to fight for the position, and fight hard, against two powerful opponents.

Septimius Severus, on the Danube, was closest to Rome and made the first decisive move. By forced marches he reached the capital (July, AD 193), overcame what opposition there was and established his authority over the Praetorian Guard. The Senate went over to him and as far as Rome was concerned it had a new Emperor. But Severus could never be effective as Emperor of the whole Empire with two ambitious opponents, and two powerful armies, still at large. Before he could begin

Opposite: The remains of the latrine at Housesteads, the south-east angle turret, and the water-storage tank in front of it.

71

to take full charge of events he had to deal, and deal decisively, with the two rival claimants to the throne. His first move was an offer to Clodius Albinus to recognise him as 'Caesar' (a title which associated him closely with the Emperor, and made him virtually heir to the throne), and to leave him in control of Britain. For Severus this was simply a breathing space in which he could deal with his other opponent, Pescennius Niger. Albinus, however, did not appear to recognise this and accepted the offer. For just over three years, from AD 193-197, he ruled Britain, not unsuccessfully, with the title of Caesar instead of his original title of governor.

During these three years Severus, acknowledged now by one of his opponents as Emperor, concentrated his energies on eliminating the other, Pescennius Niger, the claimant from the Syrian frontier. This he eventually did, and after re-organizing the eastern provinces where the trouble had originated, he turned his attention again to Britain. Declaring war on Albinus he advanced into Gaul, quite clearly intending to move against Britain itself. Albinus had two choices: to stay where he was and defend Britain with his existing troops, or to cross over to Gaul and try to win further support from the troops there. He chose the second course, crossed over to Gaul and eventually met Severus in battle at *Lugdunum* (Lyons) in AD 197. After a fierce contest Severus was the eventual victor (although he himself was nearly killed at one point), and Albinus was either executed or committed suicide. This left Severus as undisputed Emperor and he remained in office until his death (in York) in AD 211.

The events just outlined are an integral part of the history of the Roman Empire as a whole, but they are also clearly part of the history of Britain and of Hadrian's Wall. In crossing to Gaul to challenge Severus, Clodius Albinus, not surprisingly, took with him all the troops he could muster, leaving Britain, so it is said, defenceless. The northern tribes seized their opportunity and crashed through the Wall. Or did they? What may be termed the catastrophe theory has occupied an important place in the history of the Wall, not only at this time but also in the third and fourth centuries as well. In fact, the history is normally divided into four periods, the framework for which is provided by the original building of the Wall by Hadrian, *c* AD 128, and by three disasters or catastrophes in AD 197, 296 and 367. In interpreting the evidence from individual sites these events have loomed large, and the evidence has too often been fitted into the pre-conceived theory. Breeze and Dobson have recently challenged this catastrophic interpretation and suggested that the Wall was not destroyed in the way generally assumed, and that the rebuilding around the time of these events could be explained on other grounds. It is, in any case, very bad archaeological

ANTONINVS · AVG · PIVS · P · P ·

ANTONINVS, Ianuuij ortus. Imper. an.XXII.mens.VII.di.XXVI. sedens ... s. Sixto, Telesphoro, Hygino, et Pio. decessit an. Chr . CLXI.

Antoninus Pius succeeded Hadrian as Emperor in AD 138. Within a few years of his accession he had moved the northern frontier forward to a new line between the River Clyde and the Firth of Forth, known as the Antonine Wall.

practice to have virtually written the overall history of the Wall with so much evidence still to come. It makes the objective assessment of new evidence very difficult. The true history of the Wall should be the sum total of the evidence from the separate parts of the Wall. The real story will probably turn out to be a great deal untidier than the very neat sequence provided by the succession of (presumed) catastrophes in AD 197, 296 and 367.

However, in rejecting the catastrophic interpretation it is important not to swing too far the other way and completely discount any effects of the withdrawal of troops from Britain. Even if Albinus took only the legions with him, news of their

M.AVRELIVS, Roma in lucem prodit? Imper. an XIX. di XI. seder ... ib.'Pio, Aniceto, Sotere. et. Eleuthero. deces. an. Chr. CLXXX

absence from the province would probably have filtered quickly across the frontier. The tribes beyond had been aggressive enough only sixteen years before (AD 181), crossing the Wall when, as far as we know, Britain was fully garrisoned, legionary troops and all. With the legions gone, if not also some of the auxiliary troops, there must have been a considerable temptation to try again. This need not mean that the whole Wall, from end to end, was attacked. It is, in fact, very difficult to make a concerted attack on something which is over seventy miles long. What the raiding tribes probably needed most were one or two considerable breaches in the Wall, to allow them to move into the province in force and,

*Opposite: Antoninus Pius was
succeeded as Emperor by Marcus
Aurelius (AD 161-180), and under
his direction the Antonine Wall was
finally abandoned c.AD 163, having
been temporarily abandoned
c.AD 158, and Hadrian's Wall
became once more, as it was now to
remain until the end of the Roman
occupation, the northern frontier of
Roman Britain.*

most important, to get out again with their booty before the gaps could be plugged. Once a frontier system such as Hadrian's Wall is breached, and especially if the breach includes the knocking out of an auxiliary fort, then it is difficult to make good the damage quickly. No amount of patrolling across the gap can make good the deficiencies, and in any case the garrison in the adjacent forts on either side were probably fully stretched anyway with problems in their own section of the Wall. The implications of all this is that experience along the Wall is likely to have differed from fort to fort. While some forts might be damaged or completely destroyed at a particular time, others could well remain quite untouched. This is the danger of the catastrophe theory. It presupposes a series of events which uniformly affected all the forts along the Wall at the same time. If this is true, then it needs yet to be proved. So far it is only a hypothesis, with no more to commend it, in spite of its wide currency, than more recent hypotheses.

One of the arguments advanced against the catastrophe theory as far as AD 197 is concerned is the fact that the Emperor was close-by in Gaul, with an army, having just defeated Clodius Albinus. Had the frontier system been so completely overthrown as is so often suggested, then presumably Severus himself would have come over to Britain to restore the situation. The fact that he did not do so, it is argued, indicates that, whatever had happened in the province in the absence of the troops removed by Albinus, it was not sufficiently serious for any immediate move by the Emperor. Severus did eventually come to Britain, but not until eleven years later, and in very different circumstances.

We are thus faced with two opposing hypotheses. One, the traditional view, suggests that the Wall was overthrown at a stroke in AD 197 and was restored in the ten years between AD 198 and 208. In keeping with this hypothesis, the first restoration or re-building work in any fort following its original construction is attributed to this period and to the Emperor Septimius Severus. The other hypothesis is that there was no wholesale overwhelming of the Wall and that restoration and rebuilding around this time were, in fact, part of a programme of maintenance and renovation, spread over some forty years.

As ever, the truth probably lies somewhere between the two. The Wall was breached in AD 181 and this would certainly have occasioned a limited programme of restoration work. It may also have led to an inspection of the system as a whole to see if it could be improved or strengthened in any way. After all, by this time the whole system was over fifty years old, exposed to severe climatic conditions and could well have been in need of attention, possibly on a large scale. Ten years after the revolt of AD 181-7 was settled came the events of AD 196-7 and their effects, whatever they were, in Britain. In the writer's view it is unlikely that the Wall came through this period completely unscathed, although whatever happened to it probably fell a long way short of a catastrophe. The most likely pattern is damage on a varying scale, and perhaps even some destruction, at a number of places along the Wall, other places remaining completely unscathed. Such a pattern would call for restoration work in the Severan period, and again, probably, a look at the system as a whole. After all, Severus himself was a general and he made his bid for power from one of the great frontiers of the Empire, the Danube, so he was familiar at first hand with frontier problems. A great deal of work during his reign is probably to be expected, not all of it necessarily a result of prior damage and destruction in AD 197.

From inscriptions we know that work along the Wall went on during the first two or three decades of the third century. Some of this was no doubt the completion of work started under Severus, but not all of it. However, where it is not precisely dated such work tends to be attributed to him and to the period AD 198-208, as part of the restoration work following the postulated disaster of AD 197. If, however, disaster on such a scale is left out of account it is possible to see the work as part of a much wider pattern, possibly intensified in the Severan period, but nevertheless spread over some forty to fifty years. The truly objective assessment of evidence from each site, without regard to any pre-conceived catastrophe theory, might eventually enable us to distinguish those areas, if any, which really were affected by the events of AD 197. We can then, perhaps, begin to perceive just what effect the withdrawal of troops from Britain had on the northern tribes, and on the northern frontier.

Severus eventually came to Britain in AD 208, for what is generally described as a punitive expedition against the tribes who had broken through the Wall. If there had been a break through then clearly retaliation was called for. But need it have been delayed for eleven years (AD 197-208) and need it be carried out by the Emperor himself? It is usually suggested that the punitive expedition had to wait until the Wall was restored, but the period allowed for this—ten years (AD 198-208) – seems very long for a system which took only six to eight years to build in the first place. Was there, then, some other reason for the Emperor's presence? Severus campaigned in Scotland until his death in AD 211 and Roman presence there inevitably recalls the attempts to conquer the whole of Scotland in the time of Agricola and Antoninus Pius. Was this, in fact, another attempt to complete the conquest of the whole island? As described elsewhere, his work at Corbridge may have been the beginnings of a new legionary fortress which would certainly have been needed to conquer Scotland. The attempt was not necessarily for prestige. As a soldier with hard frontier experience Severus may have decided that the best solution to the northern frontier problem was to take in the whole island of Britain so that there were no land frontiers for rebellious tribes to cross. In the event this attempt too was unsuccessful and Severus died, in York, in AD 211.

After the death of Severus there appears to have been peace along the Wall for nearly a century. At least history has little or nothing to record in this period and it is generally concluded that there was, in fact, nothing to record. The Wall was presumably doing the job it was intended to do by Hadrian.

A century after the attempt made by Clodius Albinus to become Emperor, Britain was involved in another attempted *coup*. The beginnings of the episode are to be found in the raiding and piracy perpetrated by the Franks and Saxons, from beyond the Rhine frontier, against the coasts of southern and eastern Britain and northern Gaul. This reached such a pitch during the latter part of the third century that the Emperor of the West, Maximian (there were now officially two Emperors, one each for the Eastern and Western Empires), created a substantial fleet to deal with the problem. This probably incorporated the small existing British fleet, the *Classis Britannica*, which had been in existence since the early days of the conquest. The new, enlarged fleet was based at Boulogne (*Gessoriacum*), and was put under the command of an admiral named Marcus Aurelius Carausius who, like Albinus a century before, was to become very much involved in the larger politics of the Roman Empire.

Carausius was quite clearly an extremely able, not to say brilliant, naval commander and apparently had little trouble in dealing with the raiders. It was rumoured, however, that he preferred to deal with them after they had carried out their raids rather than before, so that he could relieve them of their booty, not for the benefit of the original owners, but for his own benefit and that of his seamen. Whether the rumour was true or not will never be known, although it is likely that there was at least an element of truth in it. However, because of the rumours, Maximian summoned Carausius to account for his conduct. Scenting retribution, Carausius refused to attend upon the Emperor and, not content with mere defiance, took a further bold step and proclaimed himself Emperor of Britain.

With the fleet, the three British legions, and the population at large behind him, Carausius was in a very strong position, as Maximian was soon to recognise. After several years delay while he built a fleet of his own, he challenged Carausius at sea in AD 289 and, against the experienced seamanship of the latter, almost inevitably lost. For the moment, at least, Carausius was in a stronger position than ever. With troubles in other parts of the Empire the Western Emperor Maximian and his more senior associate, Diocletian, Emperor of the East, decided to make peace, if only to allow themselves more time to deal with Carausius at a later date. Carausius was acknowledged as a colleague Emperor and left in charge of Britain and the northern strip of Gaul (the *Fretum Gallicum*, the Gallic shore of the Channel). Thus it comes about that there exist Roman coins for the year AD 289 with the heads of three emperors side by side, Diocletian, Maximian and, no doubt to the fury of the first two, Carausius.

Carausius ruled Britain for seven years, from AD 286 to 293, recognised, albeit reluctantly, as Emperor by his two associates By AD 292, however, their problems in other parts of the Empire resolved, Diocletian and Maximian, were ready to deal with Carausius. They declared war on him and put the army under the command of Constantius Chlorus, the deputy or 'Caesar' to Maximian, and father of the future Constantine the Great. Again, however, command of the sea proved the stumbling block. Against the skill and experience of Carausius and his fleet any crossing of the Channel was impossible, and if he could not be challenged in Britain, Carausius could survive indefinitely. After two years effort the only substantial result was the capture of the fleet base at Boulogne, after a prolonged siege. The stalemate was broken unexpectedly when Carausius was murdered by Allectus, the official in charge of the British treasury, to escape retribution for his own misdemeanours. Allectus took command of the province, but without the success enjoyed by Carausius. Although he ruled for three years, until AD 296, he never quite won the support of the army or the population as Carausius had done.

By AD 296, Constantius Chlorus had prepared a fleet and sailed for Britain, but the expected naval encounter never took place. Learning that he had been outflanked in a fog off the Isle of Wight, Allectus abandoned the fleet in favour of a land encounter. With an army made up of Frankish mercenaries and some, but by no means all, of the British garrison troops, he came up against Constantius Chlorus somewhere to the west of London and was decisively beaten and himself perished.

Another catastrophe? Another great overwhelming of the frontier? Another period of extensive rebuilding on the Wall and its forts? The latter .certainly, but not necessarily in response to the former. The assumption is that Allectus stripped the Wall of its troops in order to face Constantius Chlorus. But we don't know how much of the British garrison Allectus had with him when he was beaten. And if he did not have them all, the most likely absentees were those from furthest north, the auxiliary troops guarding the Wall. Even if they had been summoned by Allectus, there is no guarantee that they would have responded. Leaving the Wall unguarded would also have left their families and property without

Opposite: The Emperor Marcus Aurelius.

protection. By this time, late in the third century, they had become very much a local frontier force, and, with perhaps the exception of the younger, more ambitious men, would probably not much relish service elsewhere. The odds are, therefore, that the Wall was still manned during this episode, even if not at full strength.

However, there is little doubt that the tribes in the north would be aware of the situation in Britain and might well have decided to try their luck. Once again, however, any break through the Wall is likely to have been on a relatively narrow front, perhaps directed against a single fort and the stretches of Wall on either side. It would have been foolish of the tribes to diffuse their energies by trying to attack the whole seventy miles of the Wall at once. Again, a very careful evaluation of the evidence, both old and new, is needed to identify which forts, if any, suffered damage or destruction about this time, as opposed to those which simply show evidence of rebuilding which could have been for many other reasons. The rebuilding of the Wall is traditionally attributed to the years AD 296-306, although there is often no precise dating evidence. Once again it seems a long time for a Wall which took only six to eight years to build in the first place.

Assuming that there was some sort of break-through, then restoration work would be called for in the sector or section of the Wall involved. For the remainder of the system, however, rebuilding and restoration work around this time could well have been for other reasons. As far as the northern frontier is concerned the third century was uneventful; at least the records tell us nothing and it must be assumed that all was quiet along the Wall. Such a prolonged period of peace must have led to slackness and neglect; personal standards of conduct and performance were probably lowered, and no doubt the structural features of the frontier system suffered from lack of maintenance, aided, no doubt also, by a lack of funds from a treasury which was probably unwilling to expend its resources on a peaceful frontier. By the end of the the century a considerable amount of maintenance and rebuilding work must have become necessary, if only to save the system from complete collapse.

There was thus already a long standing need for restoration work and this may have been under way before the traditional dates of AD 296-306. The initiative to start such work may have come from Carausius himself. As a self-declared Emperor he would no doubt have felt it his duty to look to his frontiers and he may well have ordered a start to be made on bringing the Wall up to its former standard as early as AD 286. Subsequently, the presence of Constantius Chlorus in AD 296 would probably have led to a hard look at the Wall, whether damaged by enemy action or suffering simply from neglect, and no doubt this too would have stimulated further rebuilding work. Add to this the fact that an accident (due to fire or structural defect), leading to rebuilding, can happen at any time in any fort, and the possible occasions for restoration work are seen to be more numerous than is traditionally suggested where they tend to be attributed to the period AD 296-306, as necessary aftermath of extensive destruction in the Wall system.

In AD 306 Constantius Chlorus was in Britain again leading a punitive expedition against the Lowland tribes. There seems no question on this occasion that it was for punitive purposes and not for the acquisition of territory. If it was punishment for misdeeds in AD 296 then there really must have been a break through the system, although still not necessarily on a catastrophic scale as far as the Wall was concerned. The large-scale destruction would have been to the south in the province as a whole. Again, however, ten years seems a long time for retribution to be delayed. Perhaps there was some more immediate cause for a punitive campaign, some event or threat in the year or two before AD 306, of which we have no record. Whatever the circumstances, the concluding episodes of the campaign strangely echo those of a century earlier. Constantius Chlorus had reached York on his journey south when he too died, in AD 306, in the same city as Septimius Severus ninety-five years earlier.

There was trouble along the frontier again in AD 343 when the Emperor Constans, the youngest son of Constantine the Great, visited Britain in person, crossing in winter, sufficient indication that something was wrong. The Picts, aided now by the *Scotti* (originally from north-west Ireland) attacked and destroyed some of the forts beyond the Wall (the outposts), and overran the Wall itself in some places. The damage was made good, so that presumably there are parts of the Wall system with rebuilding work of AD 343 and the years following, although this is rarely allowed for in the interpretation of excavation evidence. There was further trouble in the early sixties and this was a prelude to the disasterous year of AD 367. By now Britain was being assailed by Picts, Scots, the Saxons again (quiet since the time of Carausius), and a new enemy, the Attacotti, another Irish tribe or group from the Dublin area. It was the combination of these four which led to what was probably the greatest disaster ever to befall Roman Britain.

The scale of the disaster in AD 367 can be gauged from the fact that on this occasion the Wall, as far as is known, was fully manned and that Britain as a whole was more strongly defended than ever before. A further index of the magnitude of the calamity were the deaths of both the commander-in-chief, the Duke of Britain (*Dux Britanniarum*), in charge of the northern military forces (York, Chester and the Wall), and the Count of the Saxon Shore (*Comes Litoris Saxonici*), in

SETTº SEVERO

charge of the south and east coast forts and the naval forces based there. Both were killed, apparently in the very early days of the invasion, an indication of the speed with which disaster followed disaster. From the north, east and west the Picts, the Scots, the Attacotti and the Saxons fell on Britain. The effect of these combined attacks was shattering. All organization both military and civilian broke down. People fled to the walled towns, leaving the countryside alive with marauding bands, looting, burning, pillaging, leaving death and destruction wherever they went. Even the south, so long insulated from disturbances in the north, was affected. To the inhabitants of the province it must have seemed that the end of the world had come. It was fortunate, in fact, that the raiders were motivated by a desire for booty, a long-awaited opportunity to plunder the riches of the Roman province. Had they come as invaders, with a desire for land and settlement, the subsequent history of Britain might have been very different.

The simultaneous attacks from north, east and west can surely have been no coincidence. Their speed and obvious effectiveness belie the picture of unorganized barbarian raiding parties concerned only with spoil. They imply co-ordination, planning, and a degree of discipline, and these are qualities which they must surely have acquired to some degree from their observation and experience of Roman military practice. Judging by the overwhelming success of their onslaught in AD 367 they had learned their lesson well. Roman Britain never really recovered from the blow.

Unlike the two earlier episodes, in AD 197 and AD 296, there is an historical account of the events of AD 367, by Amminius Marcellinus, a professional soldier, in his *Rerum Gestarum*, Book 27. He tells us that when news of the disaster reached the Emperor, Valentinian was, in fact, in north-west Europe, having just dealt with an incursion across the Rhine by the Alemanni. Beset with problems elsewhere, there was a considerable delay before Valentinian took any decisive action and it was not until AD 368 that he despatched the man who was eventually to restore the situation, Count Theodosius, a Spaniard, generally called Theodosius the Elder, to distinguish him from his son, Theodosius, who was to become Emperor of the Eastern Roman Empire some years later.

The first part of the re-conquest was relatively easy. The marauding tribesmen had had their own way for so long that they were probably totally unprepared for the organized military force which Theodosius brought with him, and their resistance, hampered as they were by booty and prisoners, was ineffective. The south-east was quickly cleared and Theodosius reached London which had held out against the invaders. Here he paused, his forces being insufficient for the task of clearing the rest of the country. He spent the time restoring thy civil administration in the south and gathering together the scattered remnants of many military units to add to his existing forces. The rest of AD 368 was spent in preparing for a campaign in the north with his now enlarged army. By the time he moved north in AD 369 the south was back to something like normal. By the end of the year the Roman frontier was back on Hadrian's Wall, with the raiding tribes, no doubt considerably the richer, back beyond it to the north.

There is no question that the events of AD 367 were a disaster for Britain and that the whole province was overrun. Were they also a disaster for the Wall? The co-ordinated attacks of this episode meant that as far as the east and west flanks were concerned the Wall was irrelevant. Only the northern attackers needed to get past this barrier and quite probably they did this in the same way as suggested previously, by making a breach, involving perhaps one or two forts, through which many thousands of Lowland tribesmen could pass in a very short time. With the temptation of rich booty to the south the northern tribes were not going to spend time wrecking the Wall system, even if they could have eliminated the garrisons of every fort involved. Probably at this stage much of the Wall remained intact.

However, once the scale of the disaster bacame apparent it is quite possible that troops from some of the forts and their families fled to the nearest large town, Corbridge or Carlisle. During the events of AD 367 it was unquestionably the large walled towns which fared best when it came to survival. On the other hand, the various units could probably have stayed with their families inside the forts with some degree of safety. Once the breach had been made in the system the forts, whether manned or otherwise, were largely irrelevant. If the troops left them to tackle the invaders they would leave the Wall, and perhaps more important to them, their families, unprotected, and they would probably have been swamped by sheer numbers anyway. In the circumstances survival was all, and wisdom would probably have dictated that they remain behind the ramparts of the forts. What Theodosius had to deal with when he came to restore the Wall was a wide range of conditions: forts and sections of Wall completely wrecked in the intitial onslaught; forts abandoned and perhaps looted and burned later; forts still occupied but possibly damaged by attack and, internally, probably cluttered with additional ramshackle buildings to shelter the civil population as well as the troops. Theodosius restored the Wall as the northern frontier, although it was probably now only a shadow of the system built by Hadrian. The year AD 367 was the beginning of the end for Roman Britain. The province was never the same again.

At some time in the following forty years (AD 369-410) Hadrian's Wall ceased to function as the northern frontier.

For Britain as a whole trouble piled on trouble. The main events can be outlined briefly as a background against which the end of the Wall can be seen. For about fifteen years there was peace, although probably an uneasy one. Then in AD 382 Magnus Maximus, a senior commander in Britain and a former colleague of Theodosius the Elder, made a bid for the Imperial throne, like Albinus and Carausius before him. In AD 383 he crossed the Channel and succeeded in adding Gaul, Spain and Morocco to what he had already. Although successful for a while he was eventually defeated and executed by the Emperor of the East, Theodosius, son of the Theodosius mentioned above, in AD 388. In crossing over to Gaul, Magnus Maximus inevitably took with him all the troops he could muster, seriously weakening Britain, and raids by the Irish, the Picts, and the Saxons seem to have developed on a large scale. Among the troops removed, it is suggested, were those along the northern frontier, and AD 383 is the year traditionally suggested for the end of Hadrian's Wall, although later dates have been suggested.

An early view of Steel-Rigg by Henry Burdon Richardson

The troops removed by Magnus Maximus seem never to have returned to Britain, at least not as coherent units. The much weakened province suffered badly from raids during the remainder of the century. The troubles of Britain, unfortunately, were only part of greater troubles throughout the Roman Empire and requests for help fell largely on deaf ears. Eventually, c AD 397, Flavius Stilicho listened to the British appeals. Stilicho, a famous general, had been left as regent when the Emperor Theodosius died in AD 395, in charge of his two young sons, Honorius, Emperor of the West, and Arcadius, Emperor of the East. Stilicho strengthened the defences of the province but precisely what he did in the north we do not know. If the Wall, or even the forts without the linking Wall, were still in existence then probably not much was called for there. In the circumstances, even the Wall as patched up by Theodosius, and possibly patched up again in AD 383 (if it was not entirely abandoned then), would have been something of a luxury. Any frontier defence system was better than none.

In AD 406 Britain produced yet another pretender to the Imperial throne, Constantine III. Like his predecessors he crossed the Channel (in AD 407) to make his bid for power, again taking with him all the troops he could muster. Again he was unsuccessful and was eventually defeated and executed, in AD 411. In his absence, and the absence of so many troops, raids on the province increased, and in the end, in fear and exasperation, the people of the province expelled the officials left in charge by Constantine and appealed to the Emperor, Honorius, for help, in AD 410. His reply is famous: in brief, they were to look to their own security. This, in effect, is the end of Britain as a Roman province, although the Roman shape of Britain must have endured yet for some considerable time. It is this fifth century period that we know so little about.

Thus Roman Britain fades away; apart from the advice of Honorius there is no decisive act or event which can be said to have brought the Roman period to an end. It is often said that the legions marched out, thus ending the Roman occupation. But by this time there were very few troops of any sort left to march out and what Honorius did was simply to cut the administrative ties. Rome gave up any claim to Britain, abandoning all her military and civil installations; in return she was now free of any further responsibility for the island which she had occupied for some 370 years.

The date of AD 383 has been mentioned as the generally accepted date for the end of Hadrian's Wall. The actual date, however, is possibly of less importance than the manner in which the elaborate frontier system erected by Hadrian finally ended its useful life. It is clear from a number of sites that in the final stages of occupation the forts were no longer entirely military. Granaries and even headquarters were taken over for domestic purposes and quite clearly the whole nature of the sites had changed. They were being lived in, not just by troops (if indeed the male occupants were still soldiers in the original sense), but by their families as well. Just what this means is a matter for speculation.

One suggestion is that this was a deliberate Roman act, part of a new frontier policy made necessary by the conditions of the time. The new force along the border was no longer a regular army unit but a body of frontier guards, territorial in nature, farming the area around about, and living with their families within the fort. The buildings of a traditional military establishment were no longer required, and the granaries, headquarters, hospitals, commandant's houses, etc., could be taken over for family accommodation. The date when this system came into being is equally a matter for speculation. If AD 383 is indeed the end of the Wall then presumably this is the system set up by Theodosius when he re-organized the frontier in AD 369. There are, however, other possibilities.

A move by the civil population into a fort must always be a likely possibility once the army gives up any claim to it. In the dangerous conditions obtaining around the end of the fourth century the idea of an ex-Roman army fort with its surrounding walls and internal buildings would have seemed very attractive, and the final phase of the Wall forts should, therefore, be no surprise. If this final phase was, indeed, purely a civilian one, then it is unlikely to have begun as early as AD 369. The northern frontier was certainly not given up when Theodosius was there. Indeed it has been suggested recently that the forts continued after AD 369 on more or less military lines, signs of domestic life not appearing until the early part of the next century. This suggests that the frontier system continued, in some form, after AD 383, and this, in the writer's view has always seemed a possibility. With all its shortcomings what was left of Hadrian's frontier system was better than no system at all.

In the late re-organization of Britain's defences one other name which stands out in addition to Theodosius the Elder is that of Stilicho, in the years around AD 397. It could be that the system (if indeed, it ever existed) of frontier guards-cum-farmers, living in the forts with their families, was his. He adopted more informal methods elsewhere, settling friendly tribes in North Wales who were allowed by treaty to organize themselves for defence against Irish raids. It may be that on the northern border, frontier guards, making use of existing installations, appeared to him to be the best solution, and he may, in fact, have been rationalizing something, which to a large extent, existed already.

One other possibility needs to be considered, that civilian occupation did not begin until after AD 410, until Honorius had, in effect, cut the administrative ties. The implication is that the Wall forts, in however reduced a state, remained official military installations until AD 410. When they were no longer Roman property, the civilian population moved in to begin the last stage of occupation.

The various possibilities can be summarized as follows: the purely military occupation of the forts could have ended on one of four dates, AD 367, 383, 397 or 410; if either 367 or 397 were the dates then they could have been followed by the frontier guard system, since both were dates when re-organization or strengthening of the frontier took place. If, on the other hand, either 383 or 410 was the correct date, then what followed was more likely to have been simple civilian occupation of former military sites. Like Roman Britain as a whole, the end of the Wall is obscure. There is no dramatic end; it simply fades from our view to re-emerge many centuries later as perhaps the most potent reminder of the Roman occupation of Britain.

IV

HOUSESTEADS

DEO SOLI NVIC
TBCLDECMVS
CORNELANTO
NIVS PRAEF
TEMPL RESTIT

Any account of the major features of Hadrian's Wall as it exists now must begin with Housesteads, one of the five great showplaces of the frontier. The other four are Chesters, Birdoswald, Corbridge and Vindolanda. Housesteads is situated about half-way along the Wall, between milecastle 36 (no longer visible), and milecastle 37 which still survives, about a quarter of a mile to the west. The adjacent forts are Carrawbrough to the east, nearly five miles away, and Great Chesters to the west, nearly six miles away. Housesteads stands in the rugged central sector, between milecastles 34 and 46 (a distance of 10 or 11 miles), where the Wall runs for the most part above high crags, with the ground falling steeply below to the north, making a frontal ditch superfluous. Above Winshields Crag the Wall attains its highest point above sea-level (1,230 feet), in the neighbourhood of the site of turret 40a (not preserved).

The *Notitia Dignitatum* gives the ancient name of the site as *Borcovicium*, although in an inscription the abbreviation *VER* is used. This, however, is explainable on the grounds that in the Latin of the Later Roman Empire the letters *B* and *V* were often interchanged so that the names *Borcovicium* and *Vercovicium* are both acceptable. As pronounced there was probably little or no difference in the sound. A later source, the Ravenna List of the seventh century, gives an entirely different form, *Velurtion*, but since the *Notitia* has been relied upon for the names of the other forts along the Wall, it seems best to accept its authority also for the ancient name of Housesteads: *Borcovicium*.

As at a number of other sites, there is evidence of the change of plan involved in putting the forts actually on the Wall. Within the fort, about ten or fifteen feet in from the north rampart, excavation has uncovered the foundations of the Broad Wall and of turret 36b. Although the Wall here had not gone beyond the foundation stage, the building of the turret may actually have been started since turrets and milecastles were built ahead of the sections of Wall in between. In any case, whatever stage the work had reached in this section, when the decision to change the system was made, the existing structures had to be dismantled, presumably down to ground level, to make way for the new fort. The remains of turret 36b can be seen just inside the north rampart, about 70 feet west of the north entrance.

The Wall which eventually abutted the north-east and north-west corners of the fort was the Narrow Wall (7½ feet wide), and it is clear that it was not built until the fort, or at least the fort wall, was completed. This is shown by the fact that the north-east corner turret was moved, shortly after completion, to a new position, ten or fifteen feet to the west. In its original position (the normal position in a Roman fort), the building of the Narrow Wall left it facing along the rear

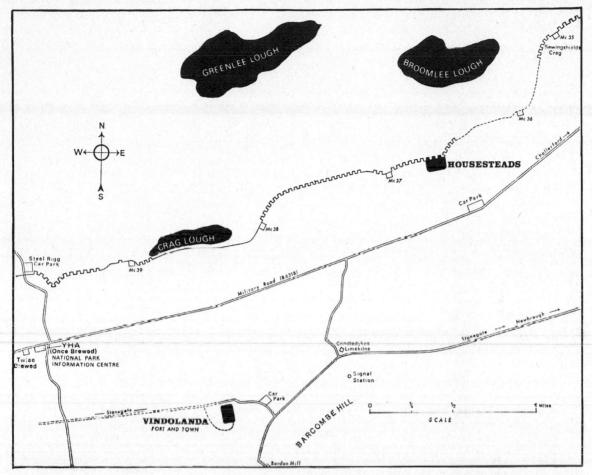

Map of the Housesteads/-Vindolanda area. Housesteads is in the central sector where the Wall runs above high crags making a frontal ditch unnecessary. The position of the Stanegate, the road from Corbridge to Carlisle, can be seen about a mile to the rear of the Wall, together with that of Vindolanda, one of the Stanegate forts.

face which, in defensive terms, is useless. There was no such problem at the north-west corner where the angle turret, in its standard position, was able to serve the needs of both the fort and the Wall at the same time.

Housesteads is situated on an east-west ridge above a point where the Knag Burn cuts through, and this, indeed, is almost certainly the reason why Housesteads was placed where it was. Because of the slope down to the stream the ground falls away to the east, although not immediately below the eastern defences. The northern defences stand above the steep northern slope of the ridge making an outer ditch superfluous. Space on the ridge top is limited, the ground beginning to slope away to the south almost from the northern edge. Because of this the fort is placed long-side on to the Wall, rather than at right angles, with its main entrance facing east behind the Wall, instead of north through the Wall, as, for instance, at Chesters or Birdoswald. The plan, moreover, is longer and narrower than usual (610 ft x 367 ft), presumably for the same reason. Even so, as the visitor will immediately notice, the whole fort slopes down to the south, so that the commandant's house is at a considerably lower level than the headquarters building to the north, and the latter is in turn at a lower level than the granaries and barrack block VII.

According to the *Notitia Dignitatum* and to inscriptions, the garrison in the third and fourth centuries was the first cohort of Tungrians, originally from the area of what is now Tongres in Belgium. However, as with most other units of this type, originally raised in other provinces of the Roman Empire, the connection with the country or area of origin was largely if not entirely nominal, particularly in the third and fourth centuries. Virtually all the recruitment was local and probably most of the auxiliary soldiers settled down, on their retirement, in the area in which they had served, with their sons, in many cases, filling their places in the ranks. The Tungrian unit is recorded in Britain some forty years before Hadrian's Wall was begun, serving with Agricola in his Scottish campaigns, and it was in Scotland again during the second century, presumably during the period when the Antonine Wall replaced Hadrian's Wall as the northern frontier. As the size and layout of the fort make clear, the First Tungrians were a large or *milliary* cohort. Although they appear always to have formed the main garrison there is also evidence that a small, irregular Frisian cavalry unit (a *cuneus frisiorum*), was stationed there in the third century, either as a reinforcement, or a replacement when the Tungrians were below strength.

Imaginative reconstruction of Housesteads fort by the late Alan Sorrell.

The defences at Housesteads consisted of a stone wall about $4\frac{1}{2}$ feet thick, backed up by an earth rampart, although the latter was mostly removed in later Roman times to make way for lean-to buildings. The stone wall was probably about 15 feet high to the rampart walk and 21 feet high overall. There was no outer ditch, except in two places, between the entrances and the Wall at the east and west ends. Elsewhere it was presumably felt that the natural slope of the ground gave as much protection as a ditch. The stone wall of the fort is well-preserved, particularly on the south and west, where the outer facing is ten or eleven courses high (6-7 feet), with the core of the wall rising another 2-3 feet.

Of the structures on the fort wall the four angle towers certainly belong to the original Hadrianic fort. The interval tower on the south rampart (between the south gate and the south-west corner) is of similar construction and is probably part of the original plan. There may well have been a corresponding tower on the north rampart. Towers in these two positions, plus the four angle towers, plus the four entrances, would have formed a symmetrical arrangement, with a tower, or twin towers roughly every 150 feet around the entire circuit, and this is probably the original Hadrianic plan. Any other interval towers are presumably later additions.

The four main gateways at Housesteads are of the standard

type, with twin portals set back between twin guard chambers. In most fort entrances, on the Wall and elsewhere, the guard chambers are carried up another storey to form twin towers. The space between, above the twin portals, forms a fighting platform at about the same level as the rampart walk. At Housesteads, however, the gates seem to have been of more

elaborate type with the whole structure carried up to tower height and the open fighting platform now at second floor level. This more elaborate type of entrance may explain the massive nature of the remains at Housesteads, which were designed to support a much heavier superstructure than usual.

In this, the first of the five forts to be dealt with in some detail, it is appropriate to say something about the actual gates and their setting in the entrance structure. The gates were of wood (oak), reinforced with iron, and were about 4 inches thick. They turned on pivots rather than hinges, and the pivot holes can still be seen in many fort and milecastle doorways along the Wall. The doors were of the two-leaf variety, opening inwards. They closed in front against a raised sill in the stone threshold and were secured on the inside by horizontal timber bars set in sockets on either side of the passage-way. The pivot-holes in the stone presumably contained an iron lining or shoe to receive the lower end of the pivot which must also have been of iron. An unlined pivot-hole would have deepened too rapidly with use and would gradually have caused the door to bear on the ground and eventually stop turning altogether.

At Housesteads, the main gate (the *porta praetoria*) was on the east side, behind rather than on the main Wall. At a late stage in the fort's history, possibly around AD 300, the south portal was blocked and converted to a guard room for the remaining single north portal. The old south guard-room became a store, its last contents, a load of coal, surviving until uncovered by excavation in recent times.

The north gate opened through the Wall. Here virtually as much of the foundations are exposed as have survived of the original above-ground structure. As it now stands the entrance looks unusable (because of the abrupt change of levels), but this is a result of the removal of the roadway immediately in front of the entrance by an early excavator, John Clayton, in 1853, his purpose being, in fact, to leave the foundations exposed, because they impressed him so much. As at the east gate one portal (the east) had been blocked, but in this case at a very early date. No pivot holes had been provided when the blocking was carried out, so presumably the north gate was never completed in twin-portal form, the east portal being blocked during the original construction in Hadrian's time.

The south gate has been much affected by later, post-Roman building. However, it is clear that, as in the north gate, the east portal had been blocked, although not at such an early date. At the south gate the blocking seems to have taken place in the fourth century possibly around AD 300, or possible AD 369.

By far the best preserved of the four main gates is the one on the west side, set in one of the best preserved sections of rampart. It stands higher than any other entrance at

Housesteads, almost up to the point where the curvature of the arches over the twin-portals began. More than anywhere else it is possible to visualize something of what the original gateway must have looked like. The west entrance seems to have remained virtually as built, with both portals open, until around AD 300 when the south portal was blocked by walls at both ends and converted into a guard chamber, freeing the original guard chamber for other uses. Later again, the north portal was blocked as well, and all the empty spaces, both portals and guard chambers filled with rubble, so that any suggestion of an entrance on the west was eliminated. This would have left three entrances, each of a single portal, in the later periods of the fort's history.

More or less complete plans of the internal buildings are known, although not all are now visible, and those that are exposed have been subject to a great deal of rebuilding so that the remains of the barrack blocks, for example, are not as clear cut as, say, the barrack blocks at Chesters. The interior can be divided into three nearly equal sections — for convenience, east, central and west. The east section, to the east of the *via principalis*, contains six blocks of barrack-like proportions, each about 160 feet long and 35 feet wide. The central section contains the headquarters building, the commandant's house, the granaries, the hospital, a workshop, and another barrack size building. The western section, the *retentura*, contained six more barrack-size blocks, although

Elevation drawing of the west gate at Housesteads. The gatehouses at Housesteads seem to have been rather more elaborate than usual. Instead of an open platform above the two portals, as shown at Chesters, for example, there was a range of rooms connecting the two towers, with the open platform above, more or less at tower height.

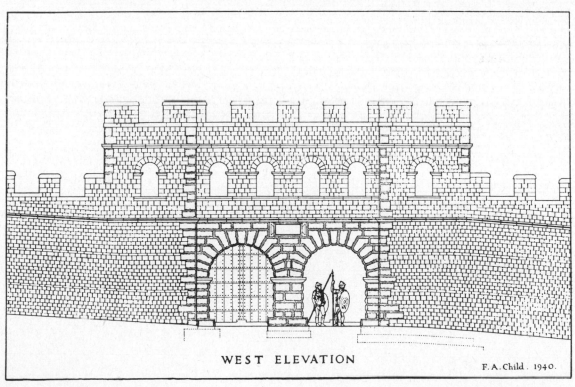

WEST ELEVATION

F. A. Child . 1940.

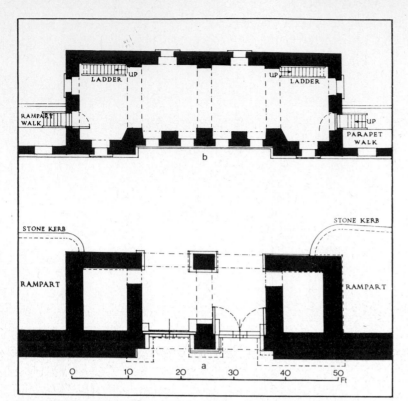

Plan of the west gate at Housesteads.

LADDER UP   UP LADDER

RAMPART
WALK

PARAPET
WALK

b

STONE KERB

STONE KERB

RAMPART

RAMPART

a

0   10   20   30   40   50 Ft

Because of the limitations of the site Housesteads lies side-on rather than at right angles to the Wall. Even so it is still very long and narrow by the standards of most auxiliary forts. The number of barrack blocks make it clear that the fort was intended to house a large or milliary *cohort, i.e. ten centuries (800 men) rather than the commoner* quingenary *cohort (480 men).*

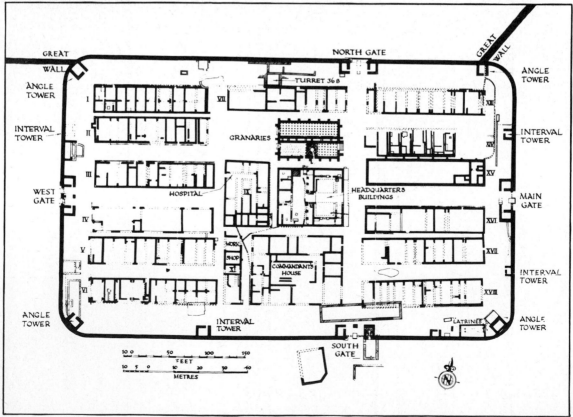

GREAT WALL

NORTH GATE

GREAT WALL

ANGLE TOWER

ANGLE TOWER

TURRET 36 B

INTERVAL TOWER

I

VII

XIII

II

XIV

GRANARIES

III

XV

HOSPITAL

HEADQUARTERS BUILDINGS

WEST GATE

MAIN GATE

IV

XVI

V

WORK SHOP XI

XVII

COMMANDANTS HOUSE

INTERVAL TOWER

VI

XVIII

ANGLE TOWER

ANGLE TOWER

INTERVAL TOWER

LATRINES

10 0   50   100   150
FEET
10 5 0   10   20   30   40
METRES

SOUTH GATE

N

General view of the headquarters.

little is visible in this part of the fort.

The garrison at Housesteads was a *milliary* cohort (800 men) so that ten of the thirteen blocks mentioned in the last paragraph must have been accommodation for the troops. Each block was normally divided into eleven sections. Ten sections were of equal size and each was designed to house eight men. A larger section at one end provided accommodation for the centurion in charge and one or two subordinates. This, however, still leaves three barrack-size blocks unaccounted for. One of them, immediately north of the *via praetoria*, was probably a mess hall, and another, in the west section, was possibly a cart-shed or a workshop. This still leaves the single block in the central sector and this may have had something to do with additional accommodation needed for the group of cavalry irregulars mentioned earlier who were stationed at Housesteads during the third century.

The main building in the central section is, as always in a Roman fort, the headquarters building, built to a standard plan. The existing remains are largely the result of the rebuilding under Septimius Severus, around AD 200, with some later additions and alterations. The remains of the earlier Hadrianic headquarters lie beneath the present building. On the east side, along the *via principalis* there was a

97

shallow portico, about 5 feet deep, which ran the whole width of the building. The entrance through this led into a courtyard surrounded on three sides by a covered colonnade, leaving the central area (*c* 50 x 30 feet) open to the sky. The rain running off the sloping roof of the colonnade dropped into a stone gutter surrounding the central area and a short section has survived at the north-west corner.

From the forecourt another entrance, in line with the first, led into the cross-hall, with additional entrances from the street at the northern and southern ends, although the southern one is no longer visible. There was a row of columns down the east side and these, together with the front walls of the rooms on the west side of the hall, supported a section of the roof which rose higher than the rest (a clearstorey), to allow for the admission of light. At one end of the hall (the north in this case) there was a tribunal or platform which would be occupied by the commanding officer when he wished to address the troops under cover.

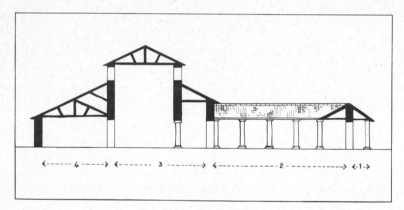

Lengthwise section of the headquarters: 1. the portico; 2. the open courtyard with surrounding colonnade; 3. the cross-hall; 4. the offices and the regimental shrine or chapel.

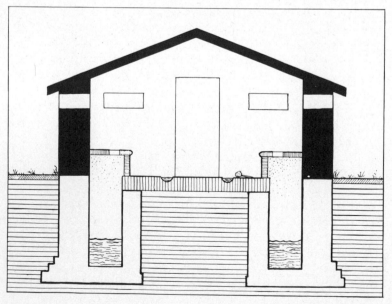

Cross-section of the latrine in the south-east corner of the fort. Water flowing in two channels below the seats on either side of the building carried the sewage away beneath the fort walls to a point down the slope some distance away.

The third part of the plan, after the forecourt and cross
hall, is the range of five rooms across the back of the building
which again can be seen in virtually all headquarters
buildings. The central room, the largest of the five, was the
regimental shrine or chapel (the *sacellum*), and contained the
standards, together with altars and sometimes a statue of the
emperor under whom the fort was built, or last re-built. The
four remaining rooms were offices, forming the administrative
centre of the fort. The two rooms to the north appear to have
been the inner and outer offices, respectively, for the adjutant
(the chief administrative officer) and his clerks, while the two
rooms to the south were probably for the standard bearers and
their staff who were also the regimental paymasters. These two
rooms often included, in addition, a strong room for the safe
keeping of regimental funds, and although there is no
surviving evidence of one at Housesteads, there is an excellent
example of the type to be seen at Chesters, where it is one of
the important surviving features of the fort.

North of the headquarters are the well-preserved remains of
two granaries, distinguished from other buildings by their
substantial buttresses. These were intended to give additional
strength to the walls against the thrust of a very strong and
heavy roof which ensured that no rain got in to damage the
grain. The other noticeable feature of the granaries are the
rows of stone piers which supported the granary floor, the

space between allowing air to circulate freely, again with the purpose of preventing damp. In fact, although two granaries have been mentioned they were built originally as a single large granary. At that time there was a row of circular columns down the centre to support the roof, and the column bases can still be seen between the two later walls. The kiln in the centre of the south granary is a much later, post-Roman feature, possibly of the sixteenth or seventeenth century.

Behind the headquarters, to the west, are the remains of the camp hospital (*valetudinarium*). This consisted of a series of rooms around a central rectangular courtyard with a covered colonnade on three sides. To the south of it a smaller building was part workshop and part bath-house (south end), for the commandant and his family, whose house was just across the narrow passageway to the east.

By far the most extensive building in the fort is the commandant's house which was, as always, immediately alongside the headquarters. Its size is probably to be explained by the fact that the officer concerned had not only himself, but also his wife, family and servants to accommodate, since it would have been normal practice to bring them with him for the duration of his service in the post. The house was of courtyard type, with four ranges of rooms surrounding the central, rectangular courtyard. There was a colonnade on three of its sides, which would have provided covered communication between the various rooms where they were not directly linked to each other by doors. The main entrance was on the east side, on the *via principalis*. A back door, at the western end, opened on to a narrow passageway, opposite the small bath-house mentioned earlier.

One interesting building remains to be described—the latrine, in the south-east corner. This is an oblong building (*c* 36 x 18 feet) with the central part of the paved floor preserved. On either side of this were two long stone benches (not preserved), with deep drains or sewers underneath, well below floor level. These carried the sewage away under the fort wall to a point some distance down the slope. In front of the benches was a stone channel in the floor with running water in which sponges (with wooden handles) could be washed, the Roman substitute for toilet paper. For this and for other purposes, water was stored in large stone tanks, one of the best examples of which is immediately adjacent to the latrine, against the inner face of the south-east angle tower. The sides are made of upright stone slabs and it was originally lined with lead to make it watertight. It measures about 16 x 10 feet and was probably originally about 3 feet deep. There are more fragmentary remains of similar tanks in other parts of the fort. There are also remains of a drainage system, much of which probably remains to be discovered. In the central area a drain runs south (i.e., downhill) beneath the headquarters and joins one issuing from the hospital and running down the passageway to the south where it must have served the needs of the bath-house on one side and the commandant's house on the other. From there it probably ran towards the south-east corner, leaving the fort by the same exit as the latrine discharge and probably helping to flush it periodically in the process. No doubt many other parts of the fort were served in the same way.

Apart from the fort itself Housesteads is also a useful base from which to see a good section of the Wall and a well-preserved milecastle, No 37. From the north-west corner of the fort the Wall runs west for just over a mile and is mostly around 4-6 feet high. For much of it the footpath is on top of the Wall and from this position one gets a very vivid, not to say alarming, impression of the situation of the Wall above the crags. In places the ground below seems to drop away in an almost sheer cliff, and this sort of siting is the dominant aspect of the Wall in this central sector. Although the foundations are certainly Hadrianic probably the upper courses are a result of one or more re-buildings in later periods. One interesting feature which can be seen in t his sector are the slight changes in the width of the Wall (about 6 inches or so), represented by offsets always in the rear face, which must be the result of different gangs working to slightly different dimensions.

About a quarter of a mile along the Wall from the fort is Milecastle 37, which contains the remains of a small barrack block, Perhaps the most striking feature of the milecastle are the remains of the original arched gateway, 10 feet wide through the Wall to the north. This was the north gate as built under Hadrian. During the reconstruction of the Wall under Septimius Severus, around AD 200, the north gate was reduced to just under four feet wide and this work is clearly visible within the frame of the original 10 foot gate. The south gate was also reduced in width at a later date; the pivot-holes of the original two-leaved gate can be clearly seen inside the gate passage. An inscription found in 1853 proves that the original milecastle was built by men of the Second Legion, from Caerleon, when Aulus Platorius Nepos was governor of the province (AD 122-6).

To the east of the fort the remains are rather less extensive. From the north-east angle the Wall runs downhill to Knag Burn and a little beyond, a distance in all of about 450 feet. Beyond this again there is little to see for about a mile until turret 35a is reached, above Sewingshields Crag. The remains of the regimental bath-house (unexcavated) are located beside Knag Burn, about 200 yards south of the Wall. As originally built there was no break in the Wall at Knag Burn, apart from the culvert necessary to allow the flow of water, but in the time of Severus (c AD 200) or Constantius (c AD 300), a gateway was provided alongside the stream for civilian as opposed to

Opposite: To the east of the fort at Housesteads the ground falls steeply to the Knag Burn where there was a gateway through the Wall for civilian traffic, controlled by guard chambers built against its south face.

Opposite: An aerial view of the fort at Chesters showing the extent of the visible remains.

Below: General view of the bath-house at Chesters alongside the river, 'the finest specimen of a military bath-house to be found in Britain'.

military traffic. Twin guard chambers were built on either side of the entrance against the south face of the Wall, with two sets of gates, at opposite ends of the entrance passage. This was probably a control feature, allowing traffic to pass through one gate, for examination and payment of tolls, before they were allowed to pass through the second.

Almost inevitably civilian settlements (*vici* pl., *vicus* sing.) grew up outside the forts along the Wall. In these were the houses for the families of married soldiers and for many a retired soldier and his wife; here were the establishments of traders and shopkeepers to supply them and the forts with the necessities of life; here also were places of entertainment and relaxation for the troops, and the many other buildings concerned with the wants and needs of a military garrison and its camp followers.

At Housesteads there was a very considerable *vicus* on the sloping ground immediately south of the fort, with an estimated population, at its peak, of some two thousand people. Little now remains above ground except for one or two structures by the south gate of the fort. One of these, however, called 'Murder House', provided some very dramatic evidence of a crime concealed until recent times. The building appears to have been a shop or a tavern, and beneath a clay floor were found buried the bodies of a man and a woman, the man with the end of a sword broken off in his ribs. Quite apart from the sword, the fact that the bodies were buried within town limits, strictly forbidden by Roman law, further indicates the commission of a crime, and also its successful concealment from the authorities. The house appears to have been built about AD 300 and abandoned around AD 367, so that the crime must have been committed between those dates. Beyond that, however, there is only speculation. On the slopes to the south, south-east and south-west of the *vicus* are a series of grass covered terraces which represent the levelling of strips of ground for cultivation. They have been proved by excavation to be of Roman date and were probably formed about the middle of the second century, a generation or so after Housesteads was first built, when the *vicus* was beginning to take shape.

This account of Housesteads can be concluded with an outline of the fort's history as far as it can be gleaned from written and excavation sources. The early history has been dealt with already. The first important event after that must have been the move forward to the Antonine Wall in the early 140s. It may be at this time that the garrison was replaced by the legionary detachment mentioned earlier, or this may be connected with the next event which must have involved Housesteads, the Brigantian revolt of AD 155. The Hadrianic Wall appears to have been re-occupied then and a certain amount of rebuilding was required (and is recorded); the legionary detachment may have been brought up for that purpose, or simply to help in settling the revolt, making use of Housesteads as a temporary base. If the sequence outlined earlier is correct then there would have been a return to the Antonine Wall fairly quickly, and after another six or seven years a final return to Hadrian's frontier, and to Housesteads, in the years around AD 163.

There was certainly a break through the Wall (presumably Hadrian's Wall), and serious trouble in the early 180s, but this does not seem to have affected Housesteads directly. However, the events which followed may have done. Ulpius Marcellus, who restored peace to the frontier, seems to have set in motion a whole series of changes in the military situation. Perhaps the rebuilding of the forts which were destroyed or badly damaged in the break through (Halton Chesters, Rudchester, and Corbridge) led to a re-appraisal of all the other forts along the Wall. Certainly during the next thirty or forty years there was a great deal of building activity along the Wall, and many changes of garrison. Many of the units which were to be associated with particular forts for the next two centuries first appeared around this time. This period includes also, of course, the attempt of Clodius Albinus to become Emperor which ended in AD 197. Whether this led to the wholesale overwhelming of the Wall (the traditional view), or to something less, are matters which have been discussed already. What is certain is that there are remains of an inscription in Housesteads museum recording rebuilding under the Emperor Septimius Severus shortly after AD 200. This could be reconstruction made necessary by the events of AD 197, or part of the general programme of renovating the forts which had begun under Ulpius Marcellus, or a combination of the two. As pointed out earlier, in discounting catastrophic destruction of the Wall it is important not to swing too far the other way and discount the possibility of any damage all. There was probably some damage to the Wall and its forts and the evidence of rebuilding suggests the possibility, and only the possibility, that Housesteads could have been one of the forts involved. The evidence is certainly not unequivocal that Housesteads and the Wall as a whole were completely overrun at this time, necessitating wholesale rebuilding.

The third century on the northern frontier seems to have been an era of peace and we have no particular evidence relating to Housesteads to suggest that events there were any different from the rest of the Wall. At the end of the century, in AD 296, came the affair of Carausius and Allectus, as a result of which the northern tribes are again deemed to have overwhelmed the Wall. There was probably some destruction and enough trouble to bring Constantius Chlorus, the Caesar or heir to the Western Empire, to Britain, but this does not imply an overwhelming disaster. Whatever the scale of the trouble, after nearly a century of peace it probably occasioned a hard look at the state of the northern defences. Discipline had probably become slack and defences allowed to run down. Some of the so-called destruction may be simply collapse due to neglect and decay. On either count—overwhelming disaster, or simply widespread neglect—there was a need for rebuilding, and there is evidence, at least at Housesteads, that rebuilding took place early in the fourth century.

Excavation of one of the barrack blocks at Housesteads has revealed a new type of accommodation for the garrison. The traditional structure (ten compartments and a centurion's quarters) was levelled and replaced by six separate closely-spaced buildings and a larger centurion's house on the same site. The six separate barrack units were about 34 x 12 feet internally (i.e., larger than the old compartments), and may have been designed to house ten men each, suggesting the possibility that by this time the century had been reduced from a complement of eighty men to one of sixty. This may be one of the results of changes in army organization which are known to have been made in the late third and early fourth centuries. Presumably other barrack blocks at Housesteads

An early view of the crags below the Wall to the west of Housesteads.

were treated in the same way, and the new-style barrack buildings were certainly built at a number of other sites as well, including Birdoswald. As part of this rebuilding work, some blocking of the gates may have taken place, as suggested earlier, although there is no direct evidence of any particular date.

In the fourth century there was trouble in AD 343 which seems to have involved the Wall, although nothing specific is known. However, the last of the traditionally 'catastrophic' events took place in AD 367. This probably was a catastrophe, but for the province as a whole and not necessarily the Wall. There was a combined attack on Britain from north east and west with raiding bands ranging far and wide, even into southern England, for so long undisturbed by events in the north. Unlike two previous occasions (AD 197, 296) the Wall appears to have been fully manned when the attack took place, and may well have survived more or less intact, being outflanked rather than broken through. Final structural changes at Housesteads are generally dated to this period, but these could just as well be the result of a review of the fortifications by Count Theodosius, as of a previous destruction. The final blocking of the gates could well be of this time.

Evidence of occupation of the Wall forts, including Housesteads, by the civilian population from the *vici* has traditionally been dated to the period of Theodosian rebuilding, after AD 369, but, in fact, much if not all of the evidence could equally well date to the period after AD 410, the end of Roman Britain as a province. Quite apart from the date, it is doubtful, in fact, if the populations of the *vici*, unless they were now very much reduced in size, could have been fitted within the ramparts of the forts. The reorganization of the frontier by Theodosius was probably still basically on military lines with Housesteads still conceived as a fort, however different from the original fort of Hadrian's time. The *vicus* may well have continued outside its walls, and perhaps only after AD 410 did some of the civilian population begin to move in and occupy quarters which were now no longer the property of Imperial Rome.

V
CHESTERS

DISCVLTO
RIBVSHVIV
LOCI IVL
VICTORITRB

Chesters is noticeably different from Housesteads, particularly in its situation. The rugged, not to say stark siting of Housesteads is replaced by (in Eric Birley's words) 'a delightful setting in one of the most beautiful valleys in Northumberland'. Chesters is situated in the eastern half of the Wall between milecastles 27 and 28, only about 400 feet to the west of the North Tyne where the Wall was carried across on a bridge, remains of which form part of the complex of structures to be seen at the site. Between the river and the fort are the substantial remains of a bath-house which served the recreational needs of the fort's garrison. In Eric Birley's words again this is 'the finest specimen of a military bath-house to be found in Britain'.

According to the *Notitia Dignitatum*, the Roman name of the site was *Cilurnum*, which in Celtic means 'cauldron', no doubt indicative of conditions in the nearby North Tyne where there was presumably a whirlpool or a section of very turbulent water. From the same source it is known that the garrison manning Chesters was the *Ala* II *Asturum*, the Second Asturian Horse, a cavalry unit 500 strong. Although no doubt originally raised in Asturias, in north Spain, it is doubtful if the unit had much connection with the original country of origin by the end of the second century. Like virtually all other units along the Wall with nominal overseas origins, filling the ranks became more and more a matter of local recruitment, so that the name, retained out of tradition, became the only indication of some much earlier connection with a distant part of the Roman Empire.

As at a number of sites along the frontier, there is evidence of the change of plan involved in moving the auxiliary forts on to the Wall. Buried beneath the fort are the foundations of the Broad Wall and of turret 27a. In front is the filled-in ditch which had evidently been completed before the change took place. The new plan meant that the ditch, turret 27a, and the foundations of the Wall had to be sacrificed before the building of Chesters could begin.

The fort was designed to hold an *ala*, the standard cavalry unit of 512 men and their horses. Chesters was built with more than a third of its area projecting north beyond the Wall, together with three of its main gates, north, east and west. This left only one main gate south of the Wall, and to compensate for this, Chesters was equipped with two additional, smaller gates, generally called postern gates, on the east and west sides.

At Chesters the visible remains are very precisely marked by fenced enclosures and the structures in them are very clearly defined. The main fort wall, visible at the angle and interval towers, was 5 feet thick and probably stood about 15 feet high to the rampart walk, with another 5 or 6 feet for the breastwork — i.e., very much the same as the Wall proper,

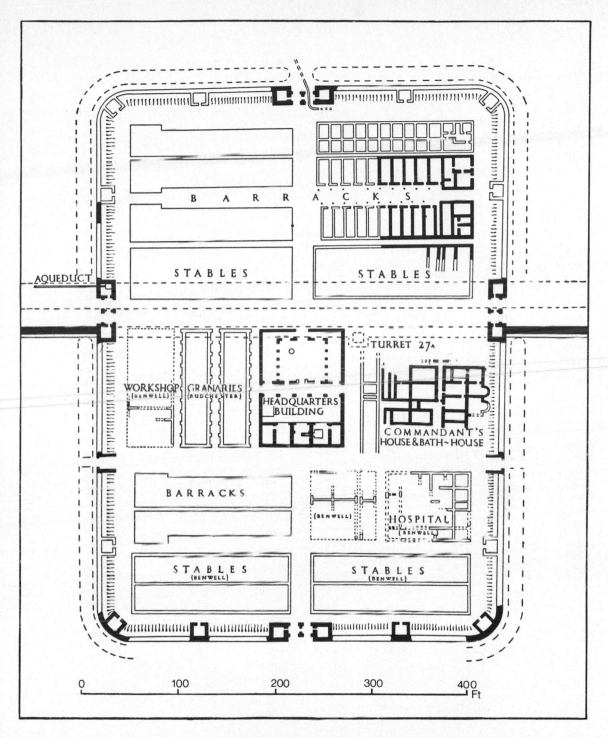

AQUEDUCT

B A R R A C K S

STABLES STABLES

WORKSHOP GRANARIES
(BENWELL) (RUDCHESTER)

HEADQUARTERS
BUILDING

TURRET 27ᴀ

COMMANDANT'S
HOUSE & BATH~HOUSE

BARRACKS

(BENWELL)

HOSPITAL
(BENWELL)

STABLES
(BENWELL)

STABLES
(BENWELL)

0   100   200   300   400 Ft

except for the thickness. However, unlike the latter, the fort
wall was backed up by an earth rampart which sloped down to
ground level at the back. In front of the wall is a V-shaped
ditch about 12 feet wide with causeways in front of the six
entrances.

(a) Restored cross-section of fort wall, rampart, and turret or postern gate; (b) restored external elevation of postern gate.

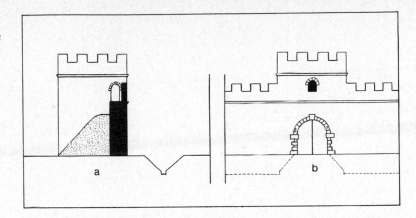

The four main gates conform to the normal plan, seen already at Housesteads: twin portals recessed between twin guard chambers which rise to form towers. At Chesters the entrance arches are set back 6 feet between the flanking towers. According to Eric Birley the rampart walk was carried across the top of the arches at a height of about 15 feet — i.e., the same height as the main rampart walk. Presumably the space between the towers and above the main entrance passages took the form of a flat roof, reached from the rampart walks on either side through the rooms above the guard chambers. This differs from the arrangement suggested at Housesteads where the space above the twin-arched portals was roofed over, presumably with a fighting platform on top at a higher level.

At the north gate the west portal was blocked at a very early date so that for the greater part of the fort's existence there was only a single (east) portal. At the east and west gates both portals had been blocked, in two stages. In the first stage all four outer archways were simply walled up. In the second stage the inner archways were walled up as well and the space between the two walls was filled up with stone. This effectively transformed these entrances into solid sections of rampart. This final blocking is possibly part of the Theodosian reconstruction after the events of AD 367. The earlier blocking, by means of walls across the outer archways, may date to a previous period of work on the Wall, around AD 300, carried out under the direction of Constantius. Prior to that date the portals of both entrances were still open, although there is not much evidence of use by wheeled traffic.

At both east and west main gates it is possible to see how the fort was linked to the Wall. Abutting the outer wall of the south guard chamber of each entrance a short section of the Wall is visible before it disappears under the general level of the field below which the greater part of Chesters fort still lies. The only other section of the main Wall visible at Chesters is a short section in a trench midway between the fort and the river on the east side.

General view of the remains of the east gate.

115

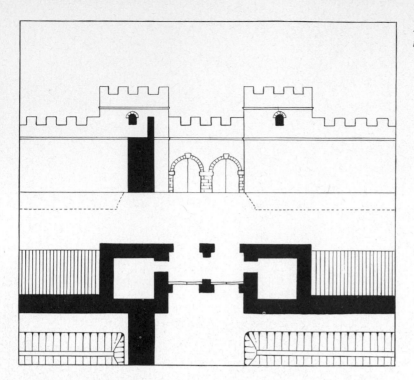

The south gate matches the one at the north in that its west portal was blocked up at a very early date. Early excavation reports record four periods of occupation in the east guard-chamber and these have, in the past, been presumed to relate to four major events on the Wall: the original construction by Hadrian; the reconstruction under Septimius Severus; the reconstruction under Constantius Chlorus; and the reconstruction under Count Theodosius. There is, however, no certainty that the relationship is so neat; some of the periods in the guard-chamber may be quite different from the accepted historic periods.

Unlike Housesteads, Chesters had two additional, smaller gates (postern gates) which had single portals and no guard chambers and were probably carried up in the form of rectangular towers above the general level of the fort wall. Since the main east and west gates of the fort were north of the Wall, the Military Way entered Chesters by the east and west postern gates.

In addition to the six gates there are four well-preserved towers along the southern side of the fort. These are about 20 feet square and consist of a single room at ground level, entered from the middle of the back wall, and probably rose about 25 feet high, with another room at rampart walk level. There was a similar arrangement at the northern end of the site, and two more towers on each of the eastern and western sides, although none of these are now visible. Including the towers above the postern gates, and the pairs of towers at each

The junction of the east gate and Hadrian's Wall. The Wall abutted the south guard chamber at both east and west gates leaving the portals of both of these entrances to the north of the Wall.

of the main gates, there were in all twenty-two towers surrounding Chesters fort.

Much of the interior of Chesters is now a pleasant, level green field, but those portions of the interior buildings which are exposed are of the greatest interest. The area north of the *via principalis* originally contained six out of the eight barrack blocks and two of the four double stable blocks. Portions of two barrack blocks facing each other are visible on the east side of this area. These were originally about 165 feet long and about 30 feet wide, except at the eastern end where there is a wider section, which provided the accommodation for the centurion. The main part of the barrack block was divided into ten compartments, each about 30 feet long and 12 feet wide and was designed to house the men of two *turmae*, six men to a compartment. Each compartment opened on to a verandah about 5 feet wide which ran along the front of the building except for the wider portion at the east end, which was already 5 feet wider than the rest. The two barrack blocks faced each other, verandah to verandah, leaving a street about 15 feet wide between with a stone-lined drain running down the centre. A small portion of a stable wall is visible to the

117

south of the barrack blocks, but not enough to show any internal detail.

The commandant's house would almost certainly have been of the rectangular courtyard type, as at Housesteads, but the visible remains at Chesters are difficult to interpret because of frequent rebuilding and alteration. It is likely that the house was rather more extensive than the present remains would suggest. The bath-house, immediately to the east, is rather more straight-forward in plan. There are four roughly equal rectangular rooms down the west side of the building and part of a fifth, the three northern rooms forming a suite. There are three more rooms beyond these, two of them having semi-circular apses on the east side. The seven rooms must have included cold, warm and hot rooms, together with a plunge bath, changing rooms etc.

The most splendid feature at Chesters is undoubtedly the headquarters building, the complete plan of which is clearly visible to the visitor. It measures 125 x 90 feet overall—i.e., very noticeably larger than the corresponding building at Housesteads. The entrance, on the north side, facing down the *via praetoria*, leads into the first part of all headquarters, the

Remains of a turret in the south wall of the fort. Such turrets, about twenty feet square, rose one storey above the general level of the fort wall.

Remains of two barrack blocks in the praetentura, *the front portion of the fort, in front of the* via principalis. *The wider portions, at the far end, were the accommodation for the centurion and his deputy.*

open courtyard with surrounding colonnade. Some of the original paving of the courtyard is still in position, a section in the north-west corner having a gutter or channel cut into it to carry away the run-off of rain from the colonnade roof.

From the courtyard three arched entrances led into the cross-hall which had a row of columns down one side forming a sort of north aisle. Two other entrances provided access from the colonnade, and two more from the streets outside to the eastern and western ends of the aisle. This range of entrances alllowed for considerable flexibility in the use of the various parts of the headquarters complex. At the western end of the cross-hall was a raised platform or tribunal from which the commanding officer could address the troops under cover. As at Housesteads the cross-hall received much of its light from a clearstorey, a raised portion of the roof supported on the columns of the north aisle and the front wall of the offices.

At the back of the cross-hall are the five standard rooms, as at Housesteads and any other auxiliary fort. The central room, the *sacellum* was the regimental shrine or chapel while the rooms on either side are generally agreed to be the administrative offices of the fort. During the Severan

reconstruction of the site a new strong room for the safe-keeping of regimental funds was built beneath the outer office of the standard bearers. The entrance was via a stone staircase leading down from the *sacellum* next door. The strong room itself had a vaulted ceiling and the stairway and the vault are well preserved and a prominent visible feature at the back of the headquarters complex. The present height of the vault makes it clear that the floor level ofthe two rooms above (the paymaster's offices) must have been raised above the general floor level when the strong room was built. When excavated around 1840 the original wooden door, reinforced with iron plates and square iron nails, was still in position although in a very decayed state.

The visible internal buildings account for only a small amount of the available internal space. The generally accepted plan of Chesters is arrived at in two ways. The area to the east of the *via praetoria* quite clearly consists of three barrack blocks and one double stable block. It seems reasonable to assume that the corresponding area to the west of the *via praetoria* was similarly occupied, thus accounting for six out of the eight barrack blocks and two out of the four

Remains of the stone paving in the open courtyard of the headquarters building, with a section of the gutter or channel around its edge to carry away the run-off of water from the roof of the surrounding colonnade.

Offices and strong room across the rear of the headquarters building

double stable blocks. In the central sector two granaries are shown west of the headquarters, in a position they are known to occupy at Rudchester, and a workshop further west again, in a position occupied by one at Benwell. In the rear section of the fort, the hospital and the two remaining double stable blocks are located on the basis of positions known at Benwell, leaving the space behind the granaries and the workshop for the two remaining barrack blocks, thus completing the disposition of all the principal buildings in the fort.

As at Housesteads a civil settlement (a *vicus*) was always a distinct possibility and early accounts mention considerable remains south of the fort. Moreover, the finding of tombstones some two hundred yards south of the fort suggested that the area in between was likely to be the area of the civilian town. This was confirmed in the dry summer of 1949 which provided excellent conditions for aerial photography. This showed a settlement of considerable extent, greater in area than Chesters itself, to the south and south-east, between the fort and the bend of the North Tyne. It also revealed the main lines of the street plan, which consisted basically of three parallel streets running south from the fort, together with two

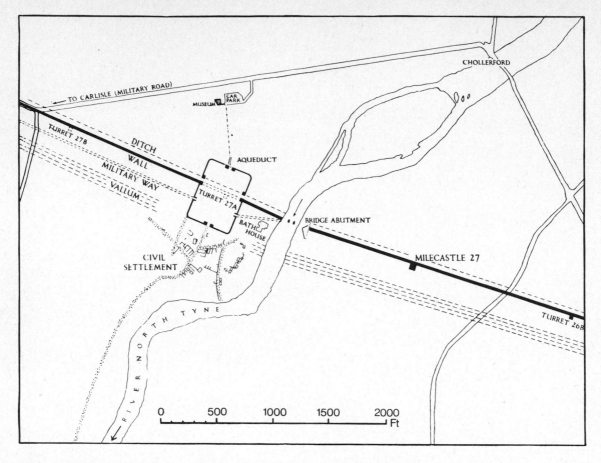

Map of Chesters and its immediate surroundings, showing the relative positions of the fort, the vicus *(civilian settlement), the bath-house, the North Tyne river and the abutments of the Roman bridge.*

cross streets, producing a slightly irregular grid pattern. A considerable number of buildings also showed up on the aerial photographs, many of them end-on to the street, a common arrangement in Roman towns; this end, often open to the front, could be a shop, or a tavern, or a workshop, with living quarters behind, and above in the case of two-storey buildings. Unfortunately, there is no surface indication of these interesting remains in the area of smooth green grass south and south-east of the fort.

The opposite is true of the second feature associated with the fort, its bath-house, a building for which Chesters is justly famous. This is situated about 200 feet to the east of the fort on the west bank of the North Tyne, and still stands to a considerable height. The bath-house was provided for the military personnel, both officers and other ranks, and as with all Roman baths, was much more than a simple bathing establishment. It was very much the garrison club, with the large changing room probably used for many other activities, such as gaming, eating and drinking. The bath-house is the result of a series of additions and modifications to an originally more modest establishment, but it will be described here in its existing state.

The entrance was at the north end, via a small porch which led into the largest room in the establishment, the changing room referred to already. Across its western end can still be seen seven round-headed recesses in the thickness of the wall, the precise functions of which are not known. They may have been for seven statues representing the guardian deities of the seven days of the week or they may have contained lockers in which valuables could be deposited while their owners were making use of the bathing facilities. From the changing room a doorway near the south-west corner led into a small lobby from which the rest of the bath-house could be reached.

The main part of the bath-house, the actual bathing section, was divided into three parts, each with its own entrance from the lobby. To the right (west) of the lobby was a suite of two rooms which provided dry heat, the first room warm, the second hot. To the left of the lobby was another suite of two rooms providing cold conditions, the first with a washing bowl at its centre and the second consisting of a cold plunge bath. Beyond the lobby to the south was the largest group of rooms, which provided moist heat, first a warm room, then a hot room, with a hot bath opening to one side of the latter. Alongside this group to the east were two more warm rooms which may be an addition to the original plan.

Plan of the bath-house. The existing plan appears to be the result of two additions to an originally much smaller establishment.

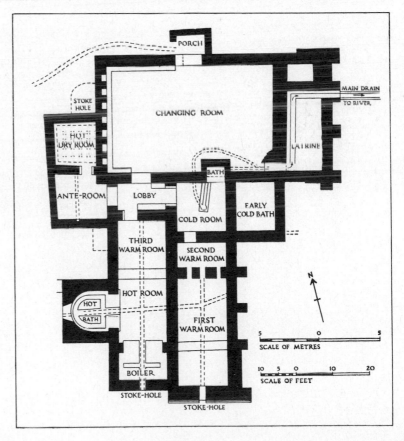

The stoke hole for the furnace at the north-west corner of the building.

The stoke-holes for the furnaces are clearly visible in the north-west angle and at the southern end of the hot moist room and the additional warm room alongside.

Beyond the bath-house on the far side (east bank) of the North Tyne are the remains of the third feature, the east abutment or foundation of the Roman bridge across the river. The river has changed its course somewhat in the last two thousand years so that the west abutment is now below river level and the east abutment is some 50 feet from the east bank. However, the west abutment and two of the three piers can be seen when the river is low. The third pier is now overlaid by the river bank on the east. The distance from abutment to abutment was 190 feet and the bridge consisted of four arches and three piers. The piers had cut-waters on their north fronts facing the direction of flow. The bridge which they carried was 20 feet wide, most of this being occupied by the Military Way, which after leaving the east postern gate of the fort gradually converged with the Wall so that both could make the crossing of the river at the same point. For structural reasons the Wall at full size is very unlikely to have been built over the bridge which probably had only a timber superstructure. There may have been nothing more than a wooden parapet to act as a continuation of the Wall walk. There appears to have been a square tower at either end of the bridge and it may be that the Wall proper terminated at these on either side.

Imaginative reconstruction of the Roman bridge.

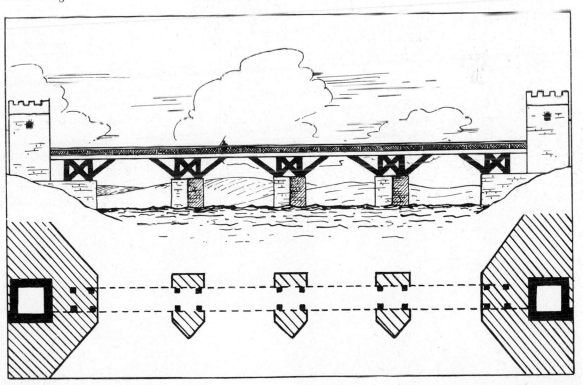

The abutment or foundation on the east bank is triangular in plan with the apex pointing west across the river. It measures about 140 feet from north to south and is built of massive blocks of stone locked together with iron clamps set in lead to avoid corrosion. It cannot be reached directly from the fort but via the foot-path along the east bank of the river from the modern bridge at Chollerford. Incorporated in the abutment is one of the piers of an earlier bridge, presumably the bridge associated with the Wall as first built. This earlier pier had cutwaters at both north and south ends and was one of four (as opposed to three in the later bridge), making five bays, forming a longer, but narrower (c 10 feet wide) bridge.

As far as the overall history of the site is concerned not a great deal can be added to what has been said already. Presumably Chesters, like other forts along the Wall, was abandoned when the move forward to the Antonine Wall took place, and was re-occupied about AD 163. Of the four periods indicated by the contents of the east guard-chamber at the south gate the second, third and fourth are traditionally equated with events in AD 197, 296 and 367. Apart from the reservations expressed earlier about the catastrophe theory as applied to these events, it must also be clear that there were other periods when building work could have taken place at the fort. One date has been mentioned already, AD 163, and to this can be added AD 180 and AD 343. An inscription of the governor Alfenus Senecio records building work done in AD 205, and this presumably equates with one of the four periods mentioned earlier, but not necessarily the second one (the first was the original Hadrianic occupation). The east and west gates were blocked in two stages and it is tempting to date these to a late period, in the fourth century when a much more defensive attitude prevailed. However, since neither entrance showed much sign of wear, it is possible that the first stage blocking took place simply when the gates had decayed through age and it was simpler to block the portals than put new gates on. In the absence of specific building inscriptions it is difficult to be more precise about the history of Chesters, even in its final phase early in the fifth century, when it probably went through the same experience as all the other forts along the Wall.

VI

BIRDOSWALD

D R S

DVPL·N·EXPLOR
BREMENARAM
INSTHNERVNT
NEIVS ᴒ CAEP
CHARITINOTRB
V S L M

Unlike both Chesters and Housesteads, which have extensive remains of their internal buildings, there is not much to see inside Birdoswald, although excavations at various times between 1851 and 1950 have established the position of the headquartes, a number of barrack blocks, and a granary, one wall of which is still visible. The chief interest of Birdoswald lies in its walls and gates, in its relationship to both turf and stone walls, which are separate.here, and in its finds, including a rich series of inscriptions on dedication slabs, altars and tombstones which tell us a great deal about the garrison of the fort, and particularly its commanding officers, during the third and fourth centuries AD. Birdoswald is also a good base from which to explore an important and informative section of the Wall, extending both east and west of the fort and including a milecastle (Harrow's Scar), several turrets, a section of the frontal ditch and an impressive stretch of the Wall itself, still standing up to eight feet in height.

The Roman name of Birdoswald is generally given as *Camboglanna*, which can be translated as 'Crooked Glen', a reflection of the fort's situation above the twisting course of the River Irthing immediately below the site to the south. This form of the Roman name is, however, something of a compromise between a number of early versions; the *Notitia Dignitatum* spells it *Amboglanna*, but this is certainly a mispelling, with the letter C omitted. Two other closely related versions are *Camboglas* and *Camboglans* (third century), while the *Ravenna Cosmography* gives the version *Gabaglanda*. Apart from the mispelling the most authoritative source is probably the *Notitia*, and this, with the support of the third century versions justifies the use of the form Camboglanna as the original Roman name of Birdoswald fort.

The situation of the fort, as indeed the name indicates, is striking, although this is not immediately apparent to the visitor approaching the site by road, who will see, for the most part, the view to the north. As one would expect with a defensive work facing north the ground does, indeed, fall away in this direction but not dramatically. The most dramatic fall is, in fact, behind the fort to the south, where the ground falls very steeply to the River Irthing, and this is true not only for Birdoswald fort but also for a three or four mile stretch of the Wall to the west. The Irthing (flowing east to west) follows a twisting course between a quarter and half a mile to the south of the Wall and between the two the ground falls very steeply, on average about two hundred feet. At first sight this would appear to be a somewhat odd position for a defensive work looking to the north, but if Hadrian's Wall was intended not only to keep out the Scottish tribes but also to contain the turbulent tribes of northern England (the Brigantes), then such a situation becomes more understandable. The Irthing

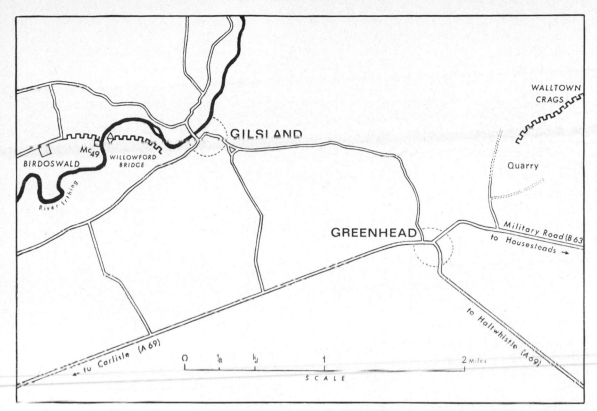

Map of the Birdoswald area showing the relative positions of the fort, Harrow's Scar milecastle and the bridge abutment at Willowford over the River Irthing.

itself, and the steep northern bank above it, would provide an excellent, natural rearward defence for the Wall against attack from the *south*, which was always a possibility, particularly in the early part of the Roman occupation.

Below the fort itself the Irthing turns through a series of bends to form a U-shaped salient to the south, leaving above it the steep-sided triangular promontory on which Birdoswald stands. In fact, the fort is set back from the end of the promontory by a distance of some 300 feet, so that even from its south wall the nature of the siting is not immediately obvious and one has to walk to the promontory edge to get the full impact of the situation. The triangular space thus defined is now featureless but it does contain, as confirmed by excavation, the early history of the site, both Roman and pre-Roman, and it is with the latter that the story of Birdoswald must begin.

When the Romans came to Birdoswald during the reign of Hadrian's predecessor, Trajan (AD 98-117) they were not the first to make use of the site. At some time in the previous century or two the native Iron Age people had built a small fort of their own, of a type fairly common throughout the British Isles known as a promontory fort. In such forts the steep natural slopes on two sides are considered sufficient defence and man-made defences are built only on the third, approachable side of the promontory. In the case of

129

An early view of Birdoswald fort.

Birdoswald, these consisted of two parallel ditches, each about 8 feet wide and about 10-12 feet apart, with the foundation trench for a timber fence or palisade about 10 feet behind the inner ditch. Although nothing now remains above ground level, the material from the two ditches must have been used to form earth ramparts between and behind the ditches, producing a defensive arrangement of a type which is relatively common in Britain: an inner rampart with a vertical timber front (the palisade), an inner ditch, an outer rampart of simple dump construction and an outer ditch. During the Iron Age period (the period immediately preceding the

Roman occupation) several thousand hill and promontory forts, some of them very big and very powerful, were built by the native population and probably underwent their final reconstruction or reinforcement as the news of the Roman advance spread. Whether this fort was still occupied when the Romans arrived at Birdoswald we do not know. They, the Romans, had already been in the area some 30-40 years, since Agricola's time back in the 80s, and it is questionable whether they would have allowed a native defensive work, even such a slight one, to remain in use under Roman rule.

At this stage Roman interest in the Birdoswald site was not concerned with the auxiliary fort, nor indeed with the Wall, which were matters for the future, but with a much less ambitious military project, the building of a signal station for which the promontory situation was well suited. To the south, just under a mile away, it formed a link with the Mains Rigg signal station alongside the Stanegate, the east-west road from Corbridge to Carlisle, established by Agricola. To the west it formed a link with the Pike Hill signal station, two-and-a-half miles away, almost exactly on the line the Wall was to follow later, while to the east, some three-and-a-half miles away, it linked with a signal station on Walltown Crags which was, in fact, later incorporated in the Wall, as turret No. 45a. It looks from this as if the Romans, long before the Wall was proposed or built, had already decided where the best vantage points lay in keeping a watch on the enemy to the north.

The Romans placed their signal station on the south-west side of the triangular promontory, within the defences of the Iron Age fort, which they presumably utilised as an outer line of protection. That the Romans were not averse to utilising pre-existing fortificiations is amply demonstrated at Hod Hill in Dorset, where a Roman auxiliary fort stands in one corner of a large Iron Age fort, making use of its ramparts on two sides and building new ramparts only on the two remaining sides. At Birdoswald the signal station within the Iron Age ramparts consisted of a rectangular enclosure, c 115 x 75 ft, defined by a ditch 4-5 feet wide which probably housed a timber fence. Of the internal structures virtually nothing is known. The troops manning the station seem to have lived in tents (made of calf skin), at least at some time during their occupation, for remains of leather tent panels were found in the bottom of one of the promontory fort ditches which seems to have been used as a rubbish dump. Presumably there was also an actual tower, or platform, for signalling, almost certainly of timber, since no stone remains appear to have been found, but beyond this little can be said. The whole area was very much disturbed by later developments when the Wall and the fort were being built.

The signal station presumably remained in use for the remainder of Trajan's reign and the first few years of

131

Hadrian's, being superseded when the next structural development on the site took place. This involved the building of the Wall but not yet of the fort, for as pointed out earlier, the original plan did not include forts, which were to be

Imaginative view of Birdoswald as it might have appeared when in use, by Alan Sorrell.

placed some distance to the rear on the Stanegate. Moreover, in this sector, west of the River Irthing, the original Wall was turf-built, as were the milecastles, but not the turrets which were from the first built of stone, in whatever sector of the

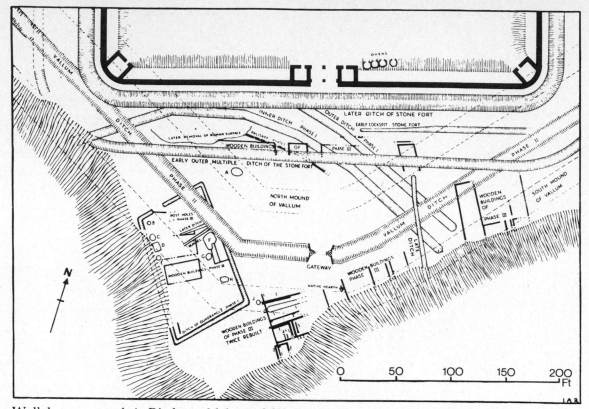

Within the image (plan labels): VALLUM · DITCH · LATER REMOVAL OF ROMAN SURFACE · INNER DITCH PHASE I · OUTER DITCH PHASE I · LATER DITCH OF STONE FORT · EARLY LOCKSPIT STONE FORT · PHASE II · OVENS · WOODEN BUILDINGS OF PHASE III · PALISADE PHASE III · EARLY OUTER MULTIPLE DITCH OF THE STONE FORT · PHASE I · A · NORTH MOUND OF VALLUM · SOUTH MOUND OF VALLUM · VALLUM · DITCH · LATE DITCH · POST HOLES PHASE III · B · LATER DITCH · BURIAL · C · D · E · F · G · H · WOODEN BUILDINGS PHASE III · WOODEN BUILDINGS OF PHASE III TWICE REBUILT · DITCH OF QUADRANGLE PHASE I · NATIVE HEARTH · GATEWAY · WOODEN BUILDINGS PHASE III · N · 0 50 100 150 200 Ft

Wall they occurred. At Birdoswald the turf Wall, running more or less east and west, was set well back from the promontory, some 400 feet north of the signal station and 600 feet from the promontory end. Details of the turf wall have been given elsewhere, and the section built at Birdoswald calls for no particular comment here. It did, however, include a turret or tower (No 49a), the remains of which now lie beneath the area occupied by the headquarters building. Had the original plan for the system been adhered to then this would have remained the extent of the defences in the Birdoswald region, with the turret now performing the signalling functions originally carried out by the signal station. The building of the turf Wall and turret 49a in the Birdoswald sector seems to have taken place in AD 123, the first full year of work on the Wall system.

Within a year or so a considerable portion of the work at Birdoswald had to be undone. It was now decreed that the auxiliary forts to house the garrison should be placed on the Wall itself, and not to the rear, on the Stanegate as originally planned. This meant that a length of the turf Wall equal to the width of the proposed fort had to be dismantled, the ditch filled in, and the stone-built turret 49a pulled down, all within a year or so of their original construction.

The fort now built into the gap created in the turf Wall was generally similar in size and layout to Chesters. As already indicated, we know very little about the interior buildings, but

Plan of the excavated area to the south of the fort, showing the remains of the Iron Age promontory fort and the Roman signal station. Nothing of these can now be seen on the ground.

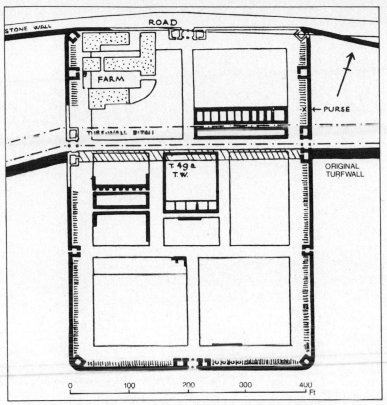

General plan of Birdoswald fort, showing the relationship to it of the (earlier) Turf Wall and the (later) Stone Wall.

we do have detailed evidence of the walls and gates, and this will be considered below, after the further changes which shortly took place at Birdoswald have been described. As it now stood the turf Wall ran up to the south guardrooms of the main east and west gates, leaving their double portals entirely north of the Wall, and these together with the main, north gateway (the *porta praetoria*) left three gates beyond the Wall, the traditional view being that these were to allow for the rapid deployment of cavalry when required in an emergency. However, it is very unlikely that cavalry ever issued from any of Birdoswald's gates.

Very soon after the fort was inserted into the Wall it was decided to replace the turf Wall with a stone Wall. Birdoswald lies in that sector (the first five miles west of the Irthing), in which the turf Wall was replaced within a year or two by a stone structure; to the east of the Irthing, of course, the Wall was stone-built from the beginning. For the most part the new stone Wall followed the same line as the turf Wall which was dismantled to make space for it. However, it was decided at the same time to make Birdoswald flush with the Wall, with only the *porta praetoria* opening to the north of it. To bring this about the new stone Wall took a different line from the turf Wall in the Birdoswald sector. Just west of Harrow's Scar milecastle the stone Wall swung away from the line of the turf Wall and made straight for the north-east corner of the fort.

135

Similarly, the stone Wall continued from the north-west corner and came back on the turf Wall line only at milecastle 51, about a mile and a half to the west of Birdoswald. This meant that the north wall of the fort was now flush with the Wall proper, instead of projecting beyond it. Whatever Birdoswald was originally planned for (cavalry or infantry) the only evidence we have indicates that it was, in fact, occupied by a *milliary* cohort and its size is consistent with this.

These two decisions brought Birdoswald broadly to the state in which we see it now, allowing for the subsequent history of the site. The fort measures 580 x 400 feet, very much the same sort of size as Chesters (582 x 434 feet) which was used as a cavalry fort for 500 men and their horses. The extra space available through using Birdoswald as an infantry fort meant that it could accommodate a large (or *milliary*) cohort—i.e., ten centuries (800 men). Whether it always housed a full complement is another matter. When the frontier moved forward to the Antonine Wall, for example, it is unlikely that Birdoswald was still manned at the same level. Then it probably contained only a skeleton force to keep the fort in commission. For the first seventy years or so we know virtually nothing of the garrison which manned Birdoswald. At the turn of the century, however, *c* AD 200, the picture changes dramatically, and a rich series of inscriptions tells us the name of the unit involved (Hadrian's Own First Cohort of Dacians), and the names, from time to time, of many of its commanding officers. These will be dealt with later.

As indicated earlier, the visible remains of Birdoswald consist almost entirely of fort walls and gates. The only remnant visible inside is the lower portion of the south wall of one of a pair of granaries situated to the west of the headquarters building. This now forms a retaining wall for the

The south wall and south gate of the fort.

garden of the farmhouse in the north-west corner of the site. The wall is some two-and-a-half feet thick and further strengthened by nine external buttresses, generally similar to the granaries at Housesteads and Corbridge.

Because it originally projected beyond the Wall, Birdoswald had six gates instead of four, the same as Chesters. At Birdoswald two of the four double-portal gates are preserved, on the south and east, and one of the two postern gates, on the west. In addition, the greater part of the rampart is preserved to between three and six feet in height, together with three of the four angle turrets and two interval turrets, north of the original turf Wall.

The fort was rebuilt on several occasions and the visible remains, therefore, tend to belong to the later rather than the earlier periods, although for the most part they were built on the same plan as previously. The remains will, in consequence, be described in general terms, without regard to period, leaving the dating of particular parts, where known, to the outline history of the site which will follow.

On the north side of the fort not much remains to be seen above ground, although there is probably much important evidence beneath the modern road. The north-east angle turret is missing, as is the north entrance and most of the northern rampart, except for a short length at the western end and around the north-west corner, where there are the remains of the north-west angle turret. The rampart runs down the west side for just over 100 feet and in this section are the remains of one of the interval towers, about 20 feet square. The west entrance and the stretches of rampart on either side have never been excavated and there is nothing visible above ground. At a point opposite the surviving granary wall the west rampart is again visible and from here, down the remainder of the west side, along the whole of the south side and most of the eastern side, rampart, gates and towers are well preserved to the heights mentioned earlier (3-6 feet).

Midway between the position of the buried west gate and the south-west corner is the west postern gate, simple in plan as compared with the main gates. It consisted of a rectangular tower, around 20 feet square, rising above the general level of the rampart, with a single portal running through it from east to west. From the west postern the rampart continues to the south-west angle and the south-west angle tower, of the same dimensions as the one at the north-west corner. Just beyond the curve, on the south face of the rampart, there are clear indications of three successive ramparts in a stepped formation, representing two rebuildings of the original fort. The first step (two courses high) probably represents the original fort as built by Hadrian. The second step (three courses high) is possibly part of the rebuilding carried out around the end of the second century, while the third step (two courses high) may be the result of further rebuilding carried out under Constantius Chlorus, *c* AD 300.

Along the whole of the south side of the fort (about 400 feet long) the outer face of the rampart is preserved to a more or less regular height of four or five courses ($2\frac{1}{2}$-3 feet), with the mortar and rubble core standing to about twice the height. Half way along are the remains of the south gate of the fort, the *porta decumana*. This is the standard twin-portal gateway, with twin guard-chambers on either side. The central portion, containing the two arched passage-ways, is set back some three feet from the front of the rampart on either side. This is normal practice and is found in virtually all the excavated forts on the Wall. What is less normal is the position of the doorways of the guard-chambers. In other forts on the wall (Chesters and Housesteads, for example) the guard-chambers open directly on to the portals—i.e., inside the arched passage ways. In the south gate at Birdoswald, however, they are in the back walls of the guard-chambers, and the same arrangement can be seen in the east gate. The east portal of the south gate appears to have been blocked soon after it was built and turned into a guard room, reducing the entrance to a single portal. This freed the original east guard room for other purposes, and indeed the remains of two ovens are visible against the south wall.

Not much of the original Hadrianic gateway remains.

Aerial view of the visible remains at Corbridge. This area (c. 400 ft. square) represents only about 7% of the town area at its greatest entent, late in the fourth century, when the town wall was built to enclose an area of some 50 acres.

Remains of the headquarter building in the western compound, showing the staircase down to the underground strongroom.

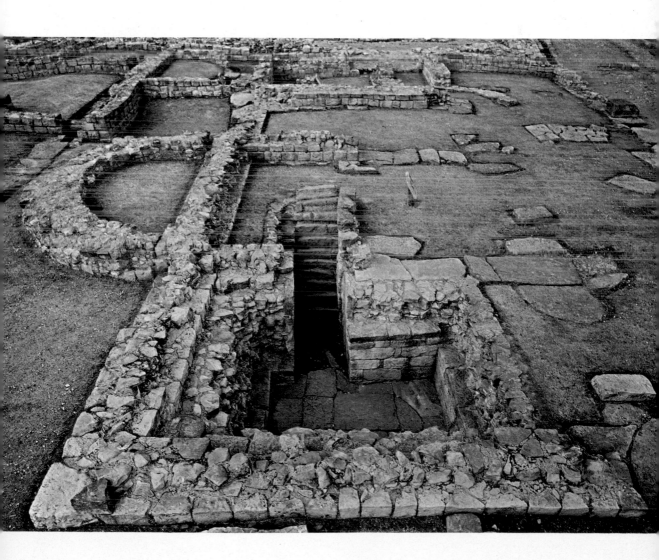

Virtually all the visible remains belong to a later period, possibly to the restoration of the frontier by Count Theodosius after the events of AD 367. This may have included the blocking of the west portal (in addition to the already blocked east portal), so that at this period the entrance went completely out of use, probably as a safety precaution, gates being reduced to the absolute minimum.

At the south-east angle the tower is preserved, although not to any great height. This angle leads round to the east side of the fort where the rampart still stands, for the most part, from eight to twelve courses high (5-7 feet), the best preserved and highest section of the whole fort. Nothing remains above ground of the east postern gate although excavation has revealed that it had been blocked at a later stage, possibly c AD 200, with the blocking renewed later, possible c AD 369.

The main east gate of the fort the *Porta Principalis Dextra*, about two-thirds of the way up the east side, is generally regarded as the most important and interesting portion of Birdoswald. Finds during excavation include a stone dedication slab recording the completion by the garrison, the first Cohort of Dacians, of restoration work on the east gate in AD 219, under the Emperor Elagabalus. However, the remains now visible belong to a still later period when the gate was again rebuilt, possibly by Constantius Chlorus, c AD 300. It was in this reconstruction that the dedication slab was re-used, as an ordinary building stone. Under the original plans, in which Birdoswald was planned to project to the north, the turf Wall ran up to the north guard-chamber, leaving the two portals north of the wall, as at Chesters. However, as pointed out earlier, this arrangement was short-lived, and when the turf Wall was quickly replaced by one of stone, the new Wall ran up to the north-east corner of the fort, leaving the east entrance some 200 feet to the rear.

The south guardroom is well preserved with three of its walls still standing about 3 feet high and the fourth, the main fort wall, to nearly twice that height. The clearly defined entrance is on the west side—i.e., opening into the fort rather than the adjacent portal. It was outside this guardroom that the dedication slab mentioned earlier was found. Although earlier foundations and lower courses were no doubt used, the visible remains are substantially the result of the further rebuilding which followed that of AD 219. In the adjacent south portal virtually the only certain remains of the original Hadrianic fort are the threshold slabs, with their pivot holes for the wooden gates which closed the portals at their outer ends.

In the original design of the east gate there were massive inner and outer central stone piers, supporting the arched passage ways of the two portals. The space between the piers was originally open allowing free movement between the two portals. In the last reconstruction, however, a wall was built

between the two piers, although a doorway was left half way along. This was because the north portal was turned into a guardroom, hence the doorway in the wall between the piers opening on to the now single, south portal. The blocking wall at the inner end of the north portal can be clearly seen in the illustration. This meant that the original north guard-chamber was now out of direct communication with the entrance. Its original entrance (on the west side), was, therefore, blocked and a new entrance was contrived into the old north portal, now a guard chamber, so that on the north side of the single portal entrance there was now, in effect, a two-roomed guard house. Again the blocking of the original north guardroom entrance can be clearly seen in the illustration. The north guardroom walls are preserved to the same sort of height as those on the south.

The remaining portion of the fort consists of the rampart and interval tower between the east entrance and the north-east corner which is, in fact, missing, together with its angle turret. The rampart in this section is ten or eleven courses high externally (*c* 6-7 feet) with the rubble core rising a foot or more higher. The interval tower, about 100 feet north of the east entrance, is well preserved with walls still standing between seven and fifteen courses high. The north-east angle and its angle-turret lie beneath the present road and there is a considerable gap (*c* 200 feet) between the fort and the long

The east wall and the east gate. The east wall is the best preserved section of the fort's defences and the east gate is the best preserved of the gates.

The view of the east gate from the inside clearly shows the blocking of the north portal which then became a guardroom and the blocked doorway of the guardroom which it replaced.

and well-preserved section of Hadrian's Wall which runs off to the east towards Harrow's Scar milecastle.

This completes the survey of the main visible features of the fort. The early events in its history have been dealt with already. As indicated earlier, we know nothing of the garrison of Hadrian's infantry fort at this time, unless it was the First Cohort of Tungrians, suggested by a tile stamp. During the occupation of the Antonine Wall it is possible that a detachment from one of the legionary bases (at York, Chester, or Caerleon) was sent to keep the fort in good order and to carry out such local duties as were still needed even with the frontier now eighty miles to the north. Although nothing to prove this has been found within the fort, inscriptions recording the presence of units of all three British legions (the Second, Sixth and Twentieth) have been found in the Birdoswald area, and in the absence of other evidence, it is a reasonable hypothesis to suggest, for the moment, that Birdoswald was occupied by legionary detachments while the frontier was on the Antonine Wall. Something similar was suggested for Housesteads during the same period, although the alternative mentioned there, that the legionary detachments were engaged on building work, is equally valid for Birdoswald.

Birdoswald may have been destroyed, or damaged, at the end of the second century when Clodius Albinus made his bid for Imperial power, but it may, on the other hand, have been rebuilt simply because by this time it was in need of rebuilding anyway. A century later the story was repeated, when on this occasion Allectus challenged Imperial authority. Birdoswald may well have been damaged (it seems unlikely to have escaped every time), although after a century repair must have been necessary anyway. It is to this period that much of what we can see at Birdoswald appears to belong, although the plan was, of course, substantially the same in all periods. In particular, we know from an inscription that the Dacian garrison restored the commandant's house, which was in ruins, the headquarters building and a bath-house, presumably the commandant's, within the fort, before AD 305, under the command of Flavius Martinus, a centurion.

Britain suffered a further disaster in AD 367 when the province was attacked from all directions. Count Theodosius was sent to restore the situation and make good the damage. At Birdoswald new ramparts, probably of this period, seem to have been built on the mixed earth and stone bank formed by the collapse of the earlier rampart, rather than on the old foundations. This means that the excavators, in clearing the site down to the ramparts as we see them now, removed virtually all the supposed Theodosian restoration, which is why so much of what we see is probably Constantian—i.e., not the last restoration, but the last restoration but one. Part of the presumed Theodosian programme was the complete blocking of the south gate, and the renewal of the blocking in the east and west postern gates. This meant that of the visible gates only one portal remained in use, the south portal at the east gate, the north portal having been blocked probably by Constantius some sixty years before. Although nothing is known of the north and west gates it seems unlikely in the circumstances that both would have been fully open, with both portals in use. It is more likely that both were reduced to a single portal, and in keeping with the more defensive attitude which became necessary during the fourth century, the north gate, opening through the Wall, may have been blocked altogether.

The (presumed)Theodosian restoration is the last structural event which we know about at Birdoswald. Its subsequent history, in the last few decades of the Roman occupation, must be bound up with the broad pattern of events described in Chapter III (pp 85-8), but we know nothing of the precise details as they relate to Birdoswald, or indeed, to any other fort along the Wall.

Two groups of finds at Birdoswald add greatly to our knowledge of the fort in particular and the Wall in general. The first group consists of two coin hoards which are important in the dating of the original fort built by Hadrian. In 1949 the remains of a bronze arm-purse were found in the ramp behind the fort wall, in the section between the east entrance and the interval tower. The purse contained twenty-eight silver *denarii* (singular, *denarius*) which indicate pretty clearly when the fort was built. Some of the coins had been minted in the Republican period, about 150 years before, and it is known that they went out of circulation in the second half of Hadrian's reign (i.e., after AD 127-128). They must, therefore, have been lost in the first half, between AD 122 when the Wall was begun and AD 127-128. The latest coins in the hoard were of Hadrian himself and, significantly, they were in mint condition—i.e., they were very new. This supports the evidence of the Republican coins that the fort was under construction early in Hadrian's reign and that during it the purse was lost by its owner. The most likely explanation is that one of the soldiers engaged on piling up the earth ramp behind the stone wall took off the purse for comfort and put it to one side, where it was accidentally buried, to be re-discovered only some 1800 years later.

For the Wall as a whole this is clear evidence that very little time elapsed between the construction of the Wall and the decision to build the auxiliary forts actually on the Wall. The second hoard, containing 30 *denarii*, was found during earlier excavations under the floor of the barrack block in the south-

Roman altars from various sites in Britain.

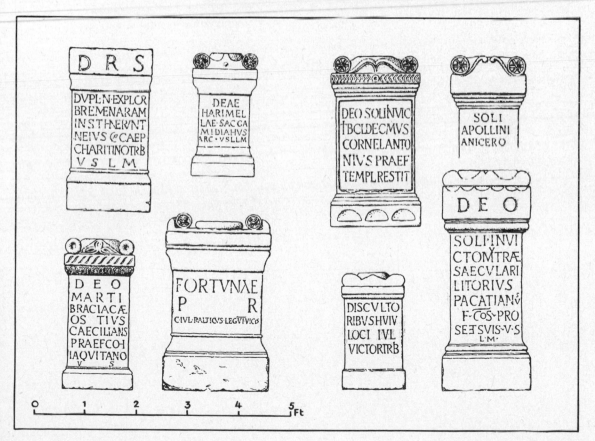

east part of the fort. This hoard contained the same range of coins as the first (Republican to Hadrianic), and proved that the barrack blocks inside the fort were likewise under construction early in Hadrian's reign. These two finds of coins leave very little room for doubt that the original Birdoswald fort was being built between AD 122 and 127, and that the decision to move the garrison forts on to the Wall was taken within the same period—i.e., very shortly after the construction of the Wall as a whole had begun. Both coin hoards are in Carlisle museum.

Imaginative view of Harrow's Scar milecastle and the Willowford bridge across the River Irthing.

The second group of finds which distinguish Birdoswald from many of the other forts of the Wall are the inscriptions on dedication slabs, altars and tombstones. They throw light on many aspects of life which can never be gleaned from structural and stratigraphical evidence alone. For example, we know the names of many of the commanding officers at Birdoswald, and their ranks, which were not always the same. An auxiliary unit such as occupied Birdoswald was normally commanded by a tribune, for example Marcus Claudius Menander, who was in charge when the rebuilding of the east

gate was completed in AD 219, or Aurelius Julianus, who was commandant a little earlier, c AD 205-208, when one of the granaries inside the fort was rebuilt. The same commandant's name appears again, in more tragic circumstances, on a tombstone which records the death of his young son, Aurelius Concordius, aged one year and five days.

However, the unit was, on occasion, commanded by a centurion from one of the legions, presumably a fairly senior one, with many years of experience behind him. For example, an altar to the god Jupiter was set up by the Dacians when they were under the command of one Julius Marcellinus, a centurion from the Second Legion based at Caerleon, and another centurion, Flavius Martinus, was in charge during the time of Constantius Chlorus when the commandant's house, the bath-house and the headquarters were restored. It should be remembered that each of the three legions in Britain contained some sixty centurions, so that there was an ample reservoir of men with great experience, particularly among the centurions of the First Cohort in each legion.

Much of the information about commanding officers and their ranks comes from a series of about twenty altars, found at different times, and as far as can be ascertained, all to the east of the fort where the garrison parade ground was almost certainly located. A new altar seems to have been put up each year alongside this, at a ceremony during which the whole garrison renewed their dedication to the welfare of the Roman Empire. Every few years the older altars were ceremonially buried in a pit alongside the parade ground, hence the fairly numerous finds at Birdoswald in the parade ground area. A similar find of buried altars was made at the Roman fort at Maryport on the Cumbrian coast. The implications are, of course, that all Roman parade grounds may be surrounded by similar caches of altars, which could write much of the history

The remains of Harrow's Scar milecastle consist of the foundations and lower courses only. Beneath these, remains of a turf-built milecastle were found during the course of excavations, this section (west of the Irthing which is immediately below Harrow's Scar milecastle) being the original turf-built part of the Wall.

of the associated fort in terms of its garrison and commanding officers.

Apart from the fort itself, Birdoswald also provides a useful centre for seeing, within a very short distance, a number of other Wall features of interest. There is an excellent stretch of Wall standing up to 8 feet high, starting about 200 feet to the east, which continues to Harrow's Scar milecastle about a quarter of a mile away. The foundations of this milecastle are well preserved, except in the south-east corner where a farm track has destroyed them. Beneath the stone walls remains of the turf-built milecastle were found during excavation, this being the original turf Wall section. In fact, immediately below Harrow's Scar milecastle to the east, at the foot of a very steep slope, is the River Irthing which marked the original boundary between the stone Wall to the east, and the turf Wall to the west. At the far side are the remains of the bridge which carried the Wall across the river. The remains consist of a tower, a stretch of Wall and the stone abutment of the bridge against the original east bank. Presumably there was a tower at each end of the bridge between which the Wall was carried on piers over the river, although whether in the circumstances it was the same height and thickness as elsewhere are matters for speculation. At full size such a Wall

The turret to the west of Birdoswald fort.

would have imposed a severe strain on the bridge piers. These remains (Willowford Bridge abutment) cannot be reached from Harrow's Scar milecastle and must be approached through Gilsland village, about 2 miles to the east of Birdoswald.

To the west of the fort the remains of the system run along the south edge of the modern road for several miles. The Wall itself continues for about a quarter of a mile beyond the fort and includes the remains of turret 49b. Beyond this it is missing but the ditch, on the north side of the road, is clearly visible for long stretches. About two miles west of Birdoswald are the remains of three turrets in fairly quick succession, 51a, 51b and 52a. The intervening milecastles are missing.

Thus, in spite of its lack of internal features, Birdoswald is an important and informative area of the Wall to visit. Apart from the fort itself, with its well-preserved east gate and good sections of rampart, there are Harrow's Scar milecastle, an excellent section of Wall in between, a long stretch of frontal ditch and a number of turrets, together with the nearby Willowford Bridge abutment, all of which amount to a very representative selection of the Wall's component features.

VII

CORBRIDGE, VINDOLANDA AND SOUTH SHIELDS

DEAE
HARIMEL
LAE·SAC GA
M IDIAHVS
ARC · VSLLM

Housesteads, Chesters and Birdoswald are integral parts of the Wall system — i.e., they are physically linked to the Wall and through it, to the associated features, the milecastles and turrets. Two of the sites to be considered in this chapter, Corbridge (*Corstopitum*) and Chesterholm (*Vindolanda*), are some distance behind the Wall to the south ($2\frac{1}{2}$ miles and 1 mile respectively), on the Stanegate, the east-west Roman road for Corbridge to Carlisle. They are, nevertheless, very much part of the Wall picture and provide two more important sites which are readily accessible to the public. They illustrate aspects of life along the Wall not covered by the three sites considered so far although, in fact, both Corbridge and Vindolanda started life as ordinary auxiliary forts no different from the other three. However, Corbridge developed eventually into a quite different type of establishment, while Vindolanda is of interest not so much for its fort as for its associated *vicus* or civilian settlement, extensively excavated in recent years, and for its full-scale replicas of sections of Hadrian's Wall, both stone-built and turf-built. Although not strictly consistent, the modern name is used in the case of Corbridge (instead of *Corstopitum*) and the ancient name in the case of Vindolanda (instead of *Chesterholm*), simply because Corbridge and Vindolanda are in both cases the better known names.

Corbridge

The existing remains at Corbridge represent something quite different from Housesteads, Chesters or Birdoswald, as virtually one glance over the site from the car park will reveal. The regular layout of the standard auxiliary fort is missing here. There is some regularity, but not of a kind encountered so far, and much irregularity, suggestive of a civilian rather than a military establishment, and this is, in fact, the key to the nature of Corbridge. Whereas Housesteads, Chesters and Birdoswald were first and foremost military sites, with associated civilian settlements (*vici*), Corbridge, at least in the third and fourth centuries, was primarily civilian, although with a still noticeable military presence, but now fitting into rather than dominating the scene. Virtually everything visible belongs to the early third century (and later), and forms part of the major reconstruction of Corbridge begun under the Emperor Septimius Severus (AD 193-211). Remains of the earlier periods are mostly buried beneath the existing structures, but excavation has yielded enough evidence to enable a brief account of the early history of the Roman site at Corbridge to be given, before dealing with the site as it stands now.

Frequent references have been made in earlier sections to the Stanegate and the Stanegate forts, built by one of the

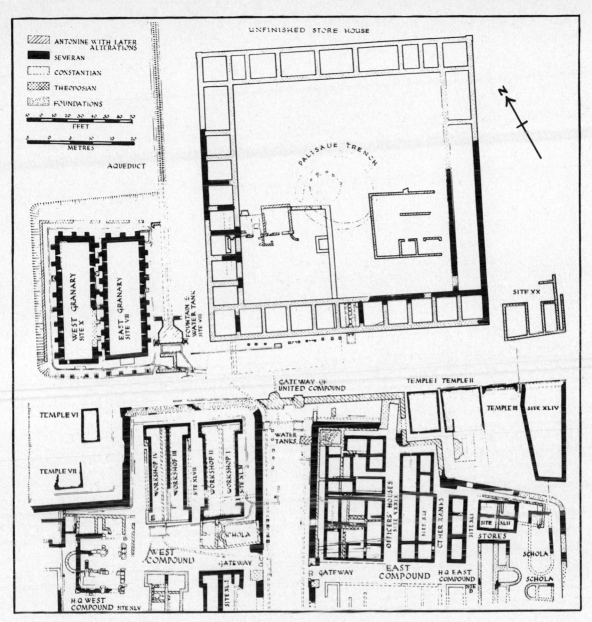

General plan of the site showing the two granaries, the storehouse, the temples and the east and west military compounds.

outstanding early governors of Britain, Cnaeus Julius Agricola (AD 78-84). Corbridge was one of the Stanegate forts, and, in fact, a rather more important one than the rest, for it was situated at the junction of the Stanegate and another important Roman road, Dere Street, the north-south route between England and Scotland. This position, at an important road junction, goes a long way to explaining the origins and subsequent development of Roman Corbridge. The north-south line of Dere Street is well established, but the Stanegate is known only from Corbridge westwards to Carlisle. Presumably it continued eastwards, ultimately, one would have thought, to the east coast, but there is at present no

155

evidence to support this, so that Corbridge must be seen on present evidence, as a three-way junction, north, south and west.

The earliest Roman structure at Corbridge ($2\frac{1}{2}$ miles south of the later Hadrian's Wall) was a fort built by Agricola in the years around AD 80. Like all forts of that period the defences were built of turf and timber, rather than stone, with timber-built internal buildings. Although the complete plan of the fort has not been established there is no reason to suppose that it was anything other than a standard auxiliary fort, little or no different from other forts along the Stanegate. This fort remained in use until about AD 124 (i.e., until it was superseded by one actually on Hadrian's Wall), but before that happened it appears to have undergone a major reconstruction following a disaster of some sort. This could have been simply a fire, started by accident, which destroyed most of the timber-built fort. It could, on the other hand, be the consequence of some larger event, affecting the region or the province as a whole. There appears to have been serious trouble in Britain very early in Hadrian's reign (AD 117-138), since there are coins indicating that it was dealt with successfully, issued shortly afterwards in the years AD 118 and 119. The trouble was almost certainly in the north and could well have involved Corbridge which was perhaps so badly damaged as to occasion the major reconstruction mentioned above. The disaster would then have taken place in AD 117 (or possibly early in 118), with the rconstruction in the following years, AD 118-120 or thereabouts. Nothing of this fort is now visible on the site.

In AD 122 Hadrian visited Britain and initiated the building of the new frontier system which we call Hadrian's Wall. Under the terms of the original plan Corbridge, together with the other Stanegate forts, was to house the main garrison of the frontier system, which at that stage consisted only of the Wall, milecastles and turrets, but no forts. Within a year or two, probably in AD 124, it was decided to move the main body of garrison troops up to the Wall itself, which meant that entirely new forts had to be built. The nearest Wall fort is Halton Chesters, $2\frac{1}{2}$ miles to the north, and this must be regarded as the Wall replacement for the Stanegate fort of Corbridge. Once the Wall forts were ready for occupation then the Stanegate forts could be abandoned, and this event indeed marks the end of the first period of occupation at Corbridge, somewhere between AD 124 and 128. During these forty odd years the garrison at Corbridge seems to have consisted of a regiment of cavalry originally raised in Gaul (the *ala Petriana*), together with a detachment of infantry from one of the three legions of Britain.

For about fifteen years, until the end of Hadrian's reign, the site was unoccupied. When Hadrian died in AD 138 his successor Antoninus Pius (AD 138-161) decided almost immediately to reverse the static frontier policy of his predecessor and to move once again into Scotland. Hadrian's Wall was abandoned as the frontier, but by the same token Corbridge came back into use. Its position on Dere Street, one of the two main routes into Scotland, on the Stanegate, which provided east-west communication with the other route into Scotland through Carlisle, and on the bridge across the Tyne, made it much too important to ignore. A new, stone fort was built at Corbridge in the years AD 139 and 140 opening the second period in the history of the site.

A little more is known of this fort than the previous one, but still not very much. The much altered remains of a small section of the headquarters building (parts of the range of five rooms at the back) have been located and are visible in the south-west corner of the later store-house. Alongside, to the east, are fragmentary remains of the commandant's house. These remains indicate that the fort faced south. It is also probable that the south, east and west ramparts coincide approximately with the edges of the Department of the Environment's enclosure around the site; the north rampart was probably a little to the north of the same enclosure. This would indicate a fort about 550 feet long and 425 feet wide, well within the size range of auxiliary forts. The headquarters building was about 122 x 84 feet with its front (south) on the east-west line of the Stanegate which is the main east-west road across the later site. This, of course, is the position of the *via principalis* in any auxiliary fort, with two of the four main gates at its eastern and western ends. It looks, then, as if the Stanegate ran directly up to the east and west gates of the second period auxiliary fort. It is also noticeable that the headquarters building faced directly down the later road between the East and West Compounds (below, pp162-3), and this must surely have been the original *via praetoria* of the fort, leading from the main (south) entrance directly to the headquarters building standing at the junction with the *via principalis*.

The date of this fort is furnished by inscriptions recording the building of granaries (beneath the existing granaries) in the years AD 139 and 140 by the Second Legion, and presumably the whole fort was complete within another year or two at most. In which case it is somewhat surprising to find further inscriptions recording extensive rebuilding in the years shortly after AD 161 under the governor Calpurnius Agricola, only about twenty years after the fort was first built. After so short an interval this cannot have been normal maintenance or renovation, and must have been occasioned by some outside event. The obvious event is the Brigantian revolt of AD 155 (above pp 64-5), during which Corbridge could have been destroyed or badly damaged, leading to the rebuilding

Overleaf: Imaginative view of Corbridge by Alan Sorrell, showing the southern range of the storehouse in use as shops, facing on to the Stanegate.

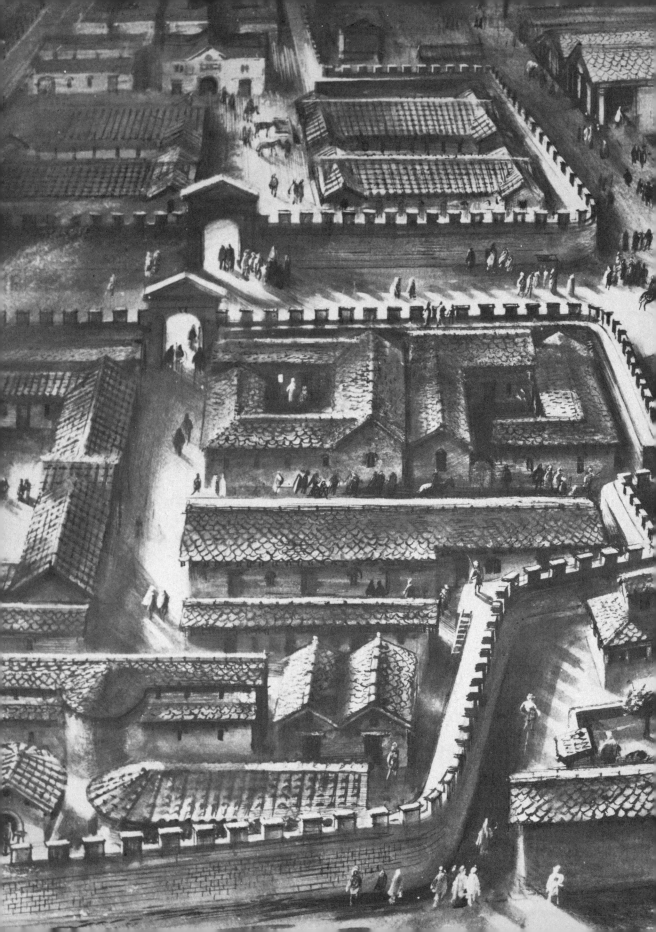

recorded above. Rebuilding of the Wall itself is recorded in AD 158 and the frontier as a whole was reoccupied around AD 163 which must have occasioned a great deal of re-building work, so that similar work at Corbridge would be entirely in context.

This brief account of the earlier history of Corbridge has now reached the point where the visible remains on the site can be brought into the story. After the reconstruction just referred to, the next event we know about at Corbridge is the extensive building work carried out under the Emperor Septimius Severus after his defeat of Clodius Albinus in AD 197. The Severan building may have been to make good destruction which resulted from the events of AD 197, but there is another possible explanation. The new buildings took an entirely different form, and were not the replacements of the standard auxiliary fort; this was a new concept, a supply base for the Emperor's campaigns in Scotland in the years AD 208-211. With Hadrian's Wall fully manned and the Brigantes quiet it may have been felt that the Corbridge auxiliary fort was superfluous. As already pointed out, however, its position at a road junction and a river crossing was strategically important, and this could have dictated the decision to build a supply base there. The extensive building work carried out by Septimius Severus is probably, therefore, to be seen not so much as a consequence of previous destruction as a logical outcome of his decision to mount large-scale campaigns against the Scots, whatever ultimate purpose he had in mind, punishment or total conquest.

The visible remains at Corbridge cover an area only about 400 feet square, and even without any additional evidence it is a fairly safe bet that such an area represents only a small part of Corbridge in its heyday, in the third and fourth centuries. The town did not have surrounding defences until a late period, but when it did, such evidence as there is suggests that they enclosed an area about 1800 x 1200 feet (c 50 acres), and this is presumably the size Corbridge had grown to by the time defences became necessary. What is visible now, therefore, represents about seven per cent of the original town at its greatest extent. The northern defences seem to have run along the line of the east-west road to the north of the site, while the western and southern defences followed the line of Cor Burn and the River Tyne respectively. The eastern defences are less easy to define but they probably ran south to the River Tyne from the sharp bend in the east-west road mentioned above, which probably curves around the north-east corner of the original town.

The site is divided into two sections by the east-west road across the site which is, in fact, the Stanegate, the Corbridge to Carlisle road. The principal features north of the Stanegate are the granaries and the so-called storehouse which was apparently never finished. The two granaries, distinguished by their massive buttresses, stand end-on to the road, on the site of the granaries referred to earlier, built in AD 139 and 140. The existing granaries were built early in the third century under Septimius Severus and rebuilt, at a later date, probably under Constantius Chlorus, c AD 300, and much of what is now visible dates to this period. The west granary is about 100 feet long and 30 feet wide, the one to the east being a few feet shorter but a little wider. They form a group not dissimilar to the one at Housesteads, where the two granaries occupied an area about 80 x 60 feet. Apart from the massive construction, common to all granaries, the most noticeable features at Corbridge are the arrangements for allowing air to circulate beneath the floors, much of which are still preserved, in the west granary in particular. In this granary the floor is supported on a series of parallel walls running lengthwise along the building, the spaces between allowing for free circulation of air. In the east granary the supports took the form of separate pillars or piers, as at Housesteads. Where it fronted the Stanegate each granary had a loading platform, covered by an extension of the roof, supported by four columns (the lower portions of which survive), forming a sort of portico, which probably formed an architectural feature in otherwise fairly plain buildings.

Beside the east granary at the roadside are the remains of a fountain which likewise appears to have had some pretension to architecture. The fountain was fed by an aqueduct from the north, but the most substantial remnant is the tank to the south into which the water flowed and from which it could be drawn as required.

Further east again are the remains of what would have been by far the largest building on the site had it been completed, the so-called storehouse. The building exists now in the form of foundations with, in a number of places, three or four courses of massive, rusticated masonry up to five feet high. In plan the structure measures 223 x 217 feet and consists of four connected ranges of buildings, about 26 feet wide, surrounding a rectangular courtyard (171 x 165 feet). In the south and west ranges the rooms are about 20 x 18 feet internally, but there is a smaller number of large rooms in the north range and only two rooms in the east range (not counting the corner rooms), the larger being about 130 feet long and 20 feet wide. There was an entrance in the middle of the south side and the rooms in the south range opened to the Stanegate. The rooms in the other three ranges seem to have opened on to the internal courtyard. In the southern half of the courtyard are the fragmentary remains of the headquarters and commandant's house of the Antonine fort built in AD 139 and 140.

This very large, albeit unfinished, building is generally described as a storehouse, part of the supply based required by the Emperor Septimius Severus for the expedition against the Scots. This may well be so, but a number of questions immediately arise. First of all, it seems too elaborate simply to support a punitive expedition which is a short term undertaking. Some more permanent function seems implied by the size and massiveness of the constructions. Although a supply base would still be required even if complete conquest were intended, once the conquest was complete it is doubtful if the same flow of supplies would be required, so even on this count a permanent storehouse seems unnecessary. On the other hand, if the whole of Scotland were to form part of the Roman province then another legionary base would probably have been required, in addition to the three existing ones at York, Chester and Caerleon, and the suggestion has been made that Severus intended Corbridge to become another legionary fortress.

Support for this view comes from the storehouse (so-called) and from evidence that there was intended to be a large attached hall to the north of it. This combination is, in fact, the formula for the headquarters of an auxiliary fort. Perhaps it was intended to use it for storage purposes while the campaign was in progress and then complete it as a legionary headquarters when there was a legion ready to move into it. Incidentally, if it was designed purely as a storehouse it would appear to have been very wasteful of space: the courtyard is much too large in relation to the covered accommodation and, in fact, accounts for most of the large area of the plan. If the cross-hall to the north was 217 feet long (the width of the courtyard building) and 70-80 feet wide, the presumed headquarters would have had overall dimensions of around 300 x 217 feet, very close to the dimensions of the other three legionary headquarters — Chester, Caerleon, and York. It may also be worth considering whether there is any significance in the fact that when it was enclosed by a town wall Corbridge enclosed about 50 acres—i.e., very much the size of a legionary fortress. Admittedly this town wall was a late feature, but could it, perhaps, have followed the line of an earlier and never completed legionary wall?

The other suggestion often made for the original function of the storehouse is that it was intended to be the forum (i.e., the main square) of the Roman town, with its basilica (hall) to the north. Forum and basilica were built very much on the same lines as legionary headquarters in terms of plan, so that this is a feasible suggestion. There are thus three possible functions: storehouse, headquarters, or forum. In the writer's view the second is the more likely. It looks as if Severus was making a final effort to conquer Scotland and if he had succeeded, another legionary base would have become a necessity, and Corbridge occupied a key position in terms of communication and would, therefore, have been a very likely choice for such a site. However, the death of Severus in York in AD 211 presumably curtailed the building of whatever was rising on the site and what the final intention was must remain a matter of speculation. The southern part of the building was eventually completed in a simpler style to serve as shops and the like, for which purpose the southern range at least, opening on to the Stanegate, was eminently suited.

Apart from some late remains to the east of the storehouse (probably shops again), the remaining structures to be considered are to the south of the Stanegate, and consist of two military compounds (east and west), later linked to become one, and the remains of a number of small temples. The compounds, surrounded by walls five feet thick, are irregular in plan, quite unlike anything encountered so far in the military sphere. This is because they were fitted in among pre-existing structures, principally temples, which the compound walls turn to avoid. The compounds face each other across the north-south street with their gateways slightly off-set from each other. It has been established that the southern wall of the east compound was some 200 feet south of the fence enclosing the visible remains, giving it an overall north-south dimension of around 350 feet. Portions of its eastern wall are visible indicating an east-west dimension of around 200 feet. The west compound, where the positions of only the northern and eastern walls are known, could well have been of similar dimensions. The southern section of each compound, away from the Stanegate and the high density of building which it was bound to create, may well have been of more regular, rectangular plan than the very irregular northern portions. At a later date, probably around AD 300, the compounds were linked by inserting a new gateway at the northern end of the north-south road between them (the old *via practoria*). Presumably there was a corresponding link at the southern end of this road, possibly with a gate or possibly just a blocking wall.

The surviving portion of the west compound consists mainly of a series of workshops, of very distinctive plan, and the headquarters building. The workshops are in groups of two, back to back and there are two complete groups on the north side of the road, and the northern halves of two more groups to the south, indicating at least eight workshops in the original plan. The intact groups are 75 feet long and 35 feet wide at the ends, which project sideways, and 28 feet wide for the main body of the building. These workshops were staffed by specialist craftsmen on detachment from two of the legions (the Second and the Twentieth), where tools, weapons and equipment were manufactured and repaired for the garrisons along the Wall. Possibly there was another such ordnance depot at Carlisle *(Luguvalium)* which seems to have served the western end of the Wall as Corbridge served the east.

The workshops are at right angles to the east-west compound road, two groups to the north and two to the south. At the western end of the road, about 100 feet from the gateway, is the compound headquarters, smaller than, but on the same lines as the rear section of an auxiliary headquarters. As originally built, early in the third century, this was about 45 x 36 feet in plan and had three entrances on the street side, a main central entrance and two lesser side entrances. These gave access to an entrance hall, offices and a central shrine (the *sacellum*). Below one of the offices is a well-preserved strongroom reached by a staircase from the *sacellum*. This headquarters is simply the office section of the workshop complex. At a later stage, probably in the time of Constantius Clorus (*c* AD 300), a semi-circular apse was added to the rear of the *sacellum*, and another suite of rooms to the north and north-east of the building.

The only other building worthy of note in the west compound is the *schola*, just to the north of the gateway. A *schola* appears to be a sort of club-house or fraternity-house, with a religious bias, where soldiers could meet and relax in their leisure hours. There are two more in the east compound, and all three seem to follow the same general plan: a rectangular main room with a semi-circular shrine at one end. The *schola* in the west compound was about 30 x 20 feet, with a semi-circular apse at its west end. Its eastern end was built into the compound wall and its entrance was actually through the wall, fronted by a four-column portico; by the time the *schola* was built, (*c* AD 300), the compounds had of course been linked together and the main gateway was now at the northern end of the roadway from which the *schola* was entered. At a later date the *schola* was extended to the west, increasing its area by more than half.

The east compound is very different in character from the west and quite clearly provided the accommodation for the personnel, both officers and men, operating in the workshop area. Two officers' houses occupy the position just inside the compound's west wall to the north of the east-west roadway. They are square in plan (*c* 48 x 48 feet) and of the courtyard type—i.e., they have a central courtyard, reached by a passage from the road outside, surrounded by seven other rooms, the smallest being about 10 x 10 feet, the largest nearly 20 x 20 feet. Subsequently the two houses were made into one and extended up to the compound wall. At a later stage again part of this building was used as a potter's workshop.

Beyond the officers' houses is what is probably a barrack block for the other ranks, about 85 feet long and 30 feet wide. A smaller block beyond, about 50 x 15 feet may also be barrack accommodation. Since the soldiers involved were legionaries their accommodation was probably based on standards in a legionary fortress where a barrack block about three times the length of the one in the east compound, and of the same width, provided accommodation for a century of 80 men and their N.C.O.s. On this basis the Corbridge block may have accommodated between 25 and 30 men with perhaps another 7 or 8 in the smaller block beyond. How many there were in the whole compound is difficult to say, but given the dimensions mentioned earlier, and assuming that the compound was largely given over to accommodation, the figures given above could be multiplied by at least three, and more likely four or five, to give a complement of about 150 men, and such a figure would fit in reasonably well with the number of workshops (probably six pairs) in the western compound.

At the eastern end of the east-west road are the somewhat fragmentary remains of the eastern headquarters building. It consists of a hall running the full width of the building, with three rooms beyond, at the back of the building, the central one, with a semi-circular apse, being the *sacellum* or chapel, and the ones at the sides being offices. Presumably this headquarters was concerned with the administration of the domestic side of life in the Corbridge military compounds. Behind it are the remains of two more *scholae* or club-houses, beyond which is the eastern wall of the compound, while to the north is a rectangular building (about 30 x 22 feet), probably for storage. The buildings south of the east-west compound road are mostly below the modern ground level and little can be said about them except perhaps that they may reflect the pattern of the buildings to the north.

The irregular layout of the north-eastern corner of the eastern compound was caused by the prior existence of buildings in this area, facing on to the Stanegate, three of them temples and the fourth of uncertain function. The temples were fairly simple rectangular structures with columned porticos, but the middle one of the group had a forecourt with the temple proper set back behind it. The fourth building, to the east of the temple, may have been a shop with living quarters and storage behind, and possibly above as well. There are remains of two other smaller temples to the west, in the re-entrant angle at the north-west corner of the western compound.

This concludes the survey of the main visible features on the site. Because of the importance of Corbridge in terms of its geographical position it is appropriate to say something about the bridge which carried Dere Street over the Tyne and into the town. The bridge consisted originally of north and south stone abutments, similar to the surviving one at Chesters, and ten stone piers, pointed at one end (the west) against the flow of the river. The superstructure was probably of wood. The road which the bridge carried was about 20 feet wide and 460 feet long. Nothing now remains to be seen except when the river is low; then the remains of the south abutment and of five of the piers are visible. The north abutment and the five northern piers are buried beneath the present north bank, probably as a result of a change in the course of the river since Roman times.

The evidence of the structural remains can be supplemented by the material on view in the excellent site museum, situated in what would have been the courtyard of the storehouse, had it been completed. Among the most important remains on display are the inscriptions referred to earlier which date certain events on the site: those of AD 139 and 140 recording work by the Second Legion; that of AD 163 recording work by the Twentieth Legion; and that recording work by the Sixth Legion in the time of Virius Lupus, the first governor of Britain under Septimius Severus after the events of AD 197. Other material includes pottery, some of it produced at Corbridge, a wide range of military equipment and horse trappings, and tools for all sorts of crafts such as leatherwork, carpentry etc. A popular exhibit is the Corbridge lion, a piece of sculpture showing a lion devouring a stag, found in the Corridor House, a large house no longer visible, on the east side of Dere Street on the slope down to the river and the bridge. Also on display is a bronze jug which, when found, contained 160 gold coins, dating from AD 64 to AD 160. These were buried beneath the floor of a house in the *vicus* or civilian settlement outside the fort, probably shortly after AD 160. Unfortunately for the owner, there seems to have been considerable rebuilding within the next few years and the precise location of the coins was lost sight of so that recovery was impossible. These coins are now in the British Museum.

The early history of Corbridge, as far as it is known, up to around AD 200 has already been outlined. For the subsequent period the history of the site is of less importance than its nature, and its relationship to the Wall and its garrison. In the development of Corbridge as it was in the third and fourth centuries (i.e., the period of the visible remains) the events of the reign of Septimius Severus are of the greatest importance. Whatever it was intended to become (a supply depot, a legionary fortress or a planned Roman town), Corbridge, already important by reason of its position, must have been a very busy place while Severus was preparing for and carrying out his Scottish campaigns, which occupied the years AD 208-210. Even the death of Severus in the following year and the abandonment of the campaign seems not to have affected Corbridge's growth, at least not permanently. Probably by this time it was too well established a part of life along the Wall for it to be in any danger of economic collapse.

Because it still had a considerable military presence, there are two aspects of Corbridge to be considered in relation to the Wall as a whole, the purely military and what may be termed the military-cum-civilian, for Corbridge, two and a half miles behind the most elaborate frontier in the Empire, could never be viewed in purely civilian terms. The purely military aspect arises out of the workshop complex, which is quite clearly something special and something more elaborate than any single fort could provide. It could not have been for any other purpose than the manufacture, servicing and repair of military equipment of all types, and this service could only have been for the forts along the Wall. Whether it served the whole Wall or only the eastern half is a matter for speculation. Corbridge is some twenty miles from the eastern end of the Wall at Wallsend and some forty miles from Carlisle, another focal point of the frontier. Corbridge could well have served as the ordnance depot for the eastern half of the Wall, covering twenty miles in either direction, while Carlisle could have performed a similar function for thy western sector.

Like any military establishment Corbridge would have attracted a *vicus* or civilian settlement around it. In fact, long before the compounds were set up, there was a civilian settlement around the then existing auxiliary fort and it was in the *vicus* of that time that the great hoard of gold coins was found. The setting up of the workshop complex probably accelerated any such development. Such an establishment would need regular supplies of many kinds of raw material and no doubt very quickly there would have grown up in Corbridge a considerable body of merchants, manufacturers, traders and middlemen to supply the workshops with what they needed. To supply these people and the troops in the compounds with the normal amenities of life (shops, taverns and other services) there must have been another section of the population, adding to the overall numbers. In addition to the compound troops, moreover, there must have been considerable coming and going from the Wall forts on military business, during which the troops would become familiar with Corbridge and what it had to offer, and no doubt this was considerably more than the *vicus* outside their own home forts. Much of this would have consisted of the family quarters of married auxiliaries, and although there were certainly shops, taverns and other amentiies, these were probably on a limited scale as compared with Corbridge which must have seemed cosmopolitan by comparison.

With a final area of about 50 acres Corbridge must have been able to offer to troops on local leave from the Wall many of the pleasures, services and relaxations which they could not get elsewhere, and it was no doubt primarily in this capacity that Corbridge flourished in the third and fourth centuries AD. The suggestion that Carlisle served the western half of the Wall as a workshop depot has already been made, although there is no proof of this. What is certain, however, is that there was a town of comparable size at Carlisle (*Luguvalium*), and it is highly probable that between them these two places acted as local leave centres and resorts where troops could get away from the routine of life on the Wall and sample some of the pleasures of civilian life. It is in this capacity, and its capacity as an ordnance depot, that Corbridge is such an important part of the frontier system and an integral part of any study or survey of the Wall.

Vindolanda

Of the sites being treated separately in these chapters, Vindolanda has attracted most attention in recent years because of the extensive excavations there, and because of the rich range of finds which add greatly to our knowledge, not only of the frontier, but also Roman Britain as a whole. The *vici* or civil settlements outside forts have been mentioned frequently, at Housesteads, Chesters, Birdoswald, and Corbridge, but not very much could be said about them, because, although some have been excavated, virtually nothing is now visible. Among the chief attractions of Vindolanda are the extensive remains of the *vicus* to the west of the fort. The other features to be seen are the fort itself, the full-scale replicas of sections of Hadrian's stone Wall (with turret), and turf Wall (with milecastle-gateway), and the museum, which contains most of the material found in the excavations in progress since 1970.

The visible remains of the fort belong to a late period (fourth century), but before dealing with this the earlier history of this part of the site, as far as it is known, needs to be dealt with, if only briefly. Like Corbridge, Vindolanda started life as one of the Stanegate forts, built by Agricola in the years around AD 80. The Stanegate lies beneath the east-west lane which runs just to the north of the site. At this date the fort would certainly have been timber-built, and remains of more than one such structure have been found beneath the existing fort and below the *vicus* to the west. In the latter area the early military remains were up to thirteen feet below present ground level, but they did produce some of the outstanding finds on the site in the way of leatherwork, textiles and writing tablets.

Like Corbridge again, Vindolanda was intended to be one of the garrison forts behind Hadrian's Wall, according to the original plan. When this plan was abandoned in favour of forts *on* the Wall Vindolanda, not unexpectedly (and again like Corbridge), seems to have gone out of use. Unlike Corbridge, however, it does not seem to have been brought back into use, as far as we know, on the move forward to the Antonine Wall (AD 139-40). It was another twenty years before Vindolanda was re-commissioned, around AD 163—i.e., at the time when there is evidence, from building inscriptions, that Corbridge was being renovated or re-modelled. The visible

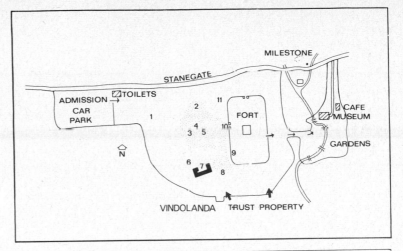

Plan of the area immediately around Vindolanda fort showing the location of the Stanegate (the road from Corbridge to Carlisle), the vicus or civilian settlement, the full-scale replicas of the stone-turf Walls and the site museum.

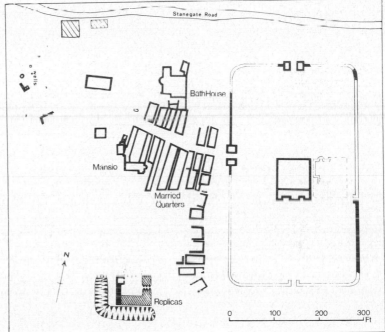

Plan of the fort and the civilian settlement outside. Most of the visible buildings face on to a street running west from the west entrance of the fort.

remains of the *vicus* also belong to this period (and later), although remains of a later and more humble *vicus* have been removed in excavation to make the earlier remains more understandable.

This fort seems to have remained in use until around AD 200 when a new fort was built, under the Emperor Septimius Severus. It is generally thought that there were two successive stone forts at Vindolanda, the one just mentioned, and the one now visible, built about a century later. Earlier forts were timber-built and Robin Birley, the excavator of the site, speaks of four such forts, although precisely how these fit into the history of Vindolanda has not yet been established. The first one must be the original Stanegate fort of around AD 80.

Opposite: General view of the remains of the headquarters. The visible remains face north, but they replaced an earlier building (of the early third century) which faced in the opposite direction.

The building of Hadrian's Wall (original plan) some forty years later, might well have prompted a complete rebuilding of the fort (No 2), still in timber, which was then abandoned on the move up to the Wall itself. Another, presumably timber, fort must have been involved in the re-commissioning of AD 163 mentioned above. At this date one would have expected a stone-built fort, but this would imply three successive stone built forts and there appears to be only two, well-accounted for. Two opposing points can be made here. On the one hand, nearly all the forts on the Antonine Wall were of timber and turf, unlike the earlier stone-built forts of Hadrian's Wall, so it is not simply a matter of dates. On the other hand, as pointed out earlier, it was in AD 163, on the move back from the Antonine Wall to Hadrian's Wall, that the turf-built western sector was rebuilt in stone, as also were the turf-built forts, Bowness, Burgh-by-Sands, Stanwix and Castlesteads. Unless the Severan fort of AD 200 was built on exactly the same lines as an earlier stone fort, it has to be assumed, on existing evidence, that the fort built in AD 163 was timber-built. A fourth fort must be fitted into the sequence somewhere but there is more than sufficient time (between AD 80 and AD 200) to fit in the four suggested timber-built forts, even if their dates are not yet precisely established

Unlike the fort now visible, the Severan stone fort faced south—i.e., the *porta praetoria* was on the south side with the headquarters facing in the same direction. The remains of this building lie beneath the visible remains of the fourth-century headquarters. Not much is known of this fort apart from its size, dimensions and garrison. It covered three and a half acres and measured 516 feet x 308 feet. Its garrison in both this and the fort which succeeded it was the Fourth Cohort of Galli (Gauls), which appears to have been a *cohors equitata*.

The third century, as far as is known, was relatively uneventful on the northern frontier and during this long period some of the forts may have been allowed to run down. However they were affected by the events of AD 296 many, if not all, of them must have been in need of a drastic overhaul by the end of the century. At Vindolanda this took the form of practically a complete re-building of the site, producing the remains which are visible today. One of the effects of this rebuilding was that the site now faced north instead of south. This is seen principally in the new headquarters, built on the remains of the old, south-facing Severan building. There was some further modification of the site, seen again principally in the headquarters, possibly in AD 369, but no fundamental changes. The visible remains of the stone fort are, therefore, mostly from the early fourth century, but with some modifications later in the century.

In plan this fort was the same as the Severan fort of a century earlier. Although the fort walls may have needed some

Opposite: The north gate, facing on to the Stanegate. The gate consists of a single portal with twin guard chambers, unlike most of the Wall forts (which are earlier) which had twin portals.

171

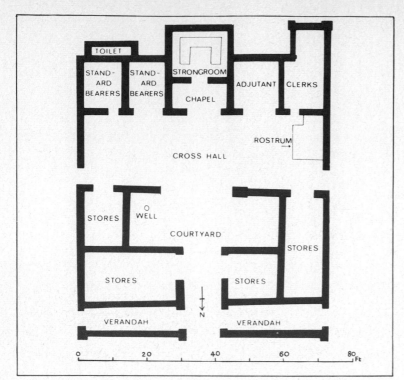

attention it is very doubtful if they would have called for complete rebuilding. The foundations and lower courses at least must be the original Severan walls. It was probably only the upper courses, and possibly the overall height, which were affected by the reconstruction. The gates, on the other hand, were probably affected by the change of orientation, particularly as both in plan and disposition they differ noticeably from the fort extrances encountered so far along the Wall. The existing south and east gates are very simple affairs, single portals without guard chambers. But the south gate was the *porta praetoria*, the principal entrance, of the Severan fort and must surely have been equipped with guard chambers, even if it had only a single portal. Changing the orientation of the fort to the north left the south gate, and the east gate also, in relatively unimportant positions and they were reduced to what in other forts have been referred to as postern gates. This change to single portals, as opposed to the earlier, virtually universal double portals, is in line with the progressive blocking of entrances, noted at one time or another, in most of the forts described so far.

The north and west gates, although likewise of single-portal type, were more elaborate in that they were both equipped with twin guard chambers which were presumably carried up above wall height in the form of towers. These were clearly the two important gates of the fort, the north one now the *porta praetoria*, facing on to the Stanegate some thirty yards away, and the west one facing into the *vicus* and one of its principal

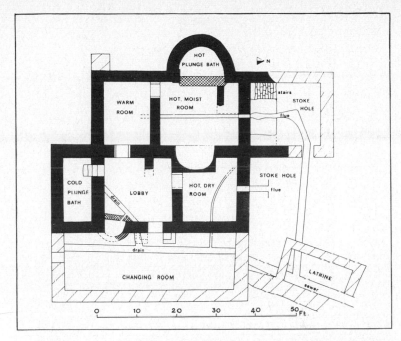

arteries, which probably converged with the Stanegate a little further to the west. This type of gate is attested elsewhere, most notably in the forts of the Saxon Shore, likewise of late date, which were built in the third and fourth centuries along the south and east coasts of England against Saxon raiding.

Another noticeable feature of the gate system in the fort is the lack of symmetry. Although there are east and west gates, not only are they different from each other, in the manner already indicated, they are also on different alignments. The west gate is, as one would expect, at the west end of the *via principalis*. There is, however, no corresponding gate on the east end, simply a blank wall. The east entrance is at the end of the *via quintana*, the east-west road behind the headquarters. When the fort faced south, however, this was the *via principalis* and the east gate was in its standard position. There was presumably a corresponding gate on the west side of the Severan fort, and the alignment of buildings in the *vicus* confirms this. The re-orientation of the fort meant that there had to be a main gate on the north and at least one gate on the new *via principalis*, and this clearly had to be on the *vicus* side, the west. These were presumably deemed adequate to cope with the major traffic in and out of the fort. There was probably now little traffic through the south and east gates which don't lead anywhere, and possibly it was felt that the existing breaks in the fort wall, stripped of extras such as guard chambers, could be retained as adequate provision for the south and east sides of the fort.

Apart from the walls and gates the chief feature of interest in the fort is the fine headquarters, built around AD 300 above the remains of the Severan building. Although on the same general lines as headquarters encountered already in other forts, there are certain noticeable differences between these and the Vindolanda headquarters. These may be accounted for by Vindolanda's late (fourth-century) date, or by the fact that it is not actually on the Wall, or by a combination of the two. It may, on the other hand, simply be that Vindolanda performed some special function which required that its headquarters should differ in certain details from other headquarters.

In plan the building measures 100 x 80 feet – i.e. larger than Housesteads, smaller than Chesters or apparently Corbridge, but of generally similar size to Birdoswald. Across the north (entrance) front was a verandah or portico, about 10 feet deep, running the full width of the building (80 feet). Behind this was the entrance proper, leading into a courtyard, open to the sky, around 47 feet long and 20 feet wide. It was around this courtyard that the Vindolanda headquarters differed from those described earlier. These usually had a colonnade on three or four sides, providing a roofed but open-fronted structure around the open court. At Vindolanda there was apparently no such arrangement. The structures around the courtyard had solid walls and formed four large rooms, apparently given over to storage. Two were about 30 x 12 feet and two about 20 x 12 feet. Although they occupy just the position a surrounding colonnade would have occupied, these rooms can hardly be a later replacement of such, since this headquarters was built, as far as we know, as it appears now. Presumably, therefore, there was a specific need at Vindolanda for this kind of storage space, or else at this time that sort of arrangement was considered more suitable where an entirely new headquarters was being built.

Beyond the courtyard the layout was broadly similar to other headquarters. There was a cross-hall, about 75 x 22 feet, running the full width of the building, with additional entrances at either end, and a tribunal or platform at the western end. At the back of the cross-hall were the usual five offices, although there was also some variation here. The central room, the regimental shrine or chapel, was larger than normal and projected beyond the back of the building. It was, in fact, sub-divided, the front portion being the chapel with the unit's strong-room behind. The rooms on either side were more or less standard, except that at some time a small room with a hypocaust (for under-floor heating) had been added to the back of the adjutant's office, and a latrine to the back of the standard-bearers' (paymasters') offices, forming two more projections beyond the normally straight back wall of the headquarters building.

Late changes in the building are generally attributed to Theodosius and the years AD 369-70. These, it is suggested,

The stone water tank and the site of the fountain at Corbridge.

The Corbridge Lion. The subject of the sculpture is a lion devouring a stag, a popular Roman theme. The piece was, in fact, a fountain head, from the Corridor House (not now visible) which was situated on the slope between the excavated area and the river.

involve the conversion of the offices to living quarters by the addition of hypocausts for under-floor heading. This is in keeping with the long-held theory that after the events of AD 367 the inhabitants of the *vici* moved into the forts with the garrison for greater safety. As pointed out earlier, this view has recently been questioned by Breeze and Dobson who suggest that such occupation probably belongs to a later period still, when the administrative ties with Rome had been finally severed. The final days of Vindolanda, as indeed of virtually all the forts along the Wall, are still somewhat obscure, and must await the evidence of future excavations.

Beyond the fort to the west are the remains of the *vicus*, the main concentration being outside the west gate. As pointed out earlier, the buildings front on to a road leading from the west gate and swinging towards the north-west, presumably to join the Stanegate a little further west. The southern ends of a number of buildings on the south side of this road also end in line with each other, indicating another road, running west from where an earlier west gate would have been. A presumably later building across its eastern end suggests that at some stage it ceased to be a main artery, possibly when the old west entrance went out of use. The principal buildings in the *vicus* are the bath-house, the *mansio* or inn, the corridor house and the married quarters block for the families of married soldiers.

The bath-house was, at first, probably a military bath-house, for the recreation of the garrison, but later it appears to have served both military and civilian needs. It was on a rather smaller scale than the one described earlier at Chesters, but followed the same general arrangement. A changing room running the full width of the building gave access to a central lobby, from which the different parts of the bath could be reached. To the left of the lobby a doorway and a few steps led down to a cold plunge bath. A doorway on the right led into a hot dry room. At the back of the lobby another door led into the main suite of rooms, a warm room, leading into a hot, but this time moist, room with a hot plunge bath contained in a semi-circular recess to one side. Stamped bricks indicate that the bath-house was built by a detachment of the Sixth Legion from York, probably between AD 163 when the fort was re-commissioned and AD 200 when the first stone fort was built.

A small bathing establishment was also included in possibly the most interesting building at Vindolanda, and one of a type not encountered so far along the Wall, the *mansio* or inn for travellers. This was situated on the south side of the road from the west gate and consisted basically of a long narrow courtyard with ranges of rooms on three sides and a wall, with an entrance, on the fourth side, facing on to the road. The courtyard was about 45 x 15 feet with the entrance in the middle of one of the shorter sides. On each of the long sides

General view of the mansio *or inn from the south.*

there were half a dozen rooms, six of them apparently guest rooms (quite small, about 7 feet square), and the rest the sort of rooms to be expected in an inn or hotel: a dining room, a kitchen, a latrine, a stoke house (for the baths), plus a room of unknown purpose. Across the back of the courtyard was a larger building which was possibly of more than one storey. It contained a central entrance lobby with a small baths complex to the left and a room to the right described as a changing room, but this, in the manner of changing rooms in bath-houses, may have served also as a club or gaming room, for relaxation, serving both the needs of the bath-house and the inn. There may well have been further accommodation for guests on the upper floor of this building. The irregular plan suggests that this end block and the two long side ranges were built at different times, with the end block probably the earlier, in which case it looks as if the inn could have grown out of an original bathing establishment as the need for short-term accommodation developed. An adjacent entrance gave access to a long narrow stable yard with a range of stables and servants quarters along one side facing the back wall of the range of rooms down the east side of the main courtyard.

Diagonally across the road from the *mansio* are the remains

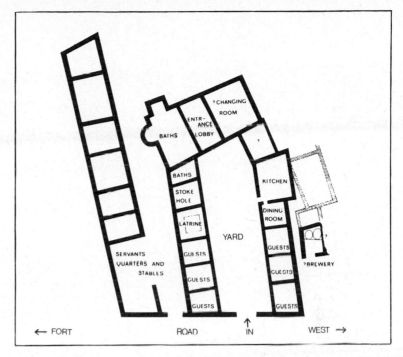

Plan of the mansio. *The buildings were grouped around an open courtyard with access from the street at the north end via a gate through the wall. The main communal buildings were at the opposite end of the courtyard.*

of a large private house (about 50 x 40 feet), known as the Corridor House. This consisted of a central corridor running from front to back with three rooms on each side. Not all of these were part of the living accommodation. To judge from the number of drains serving it, one of the rooms (to the left of the entrance), was a butcher's shop which would have been quite separate from the house, opening directly on to the street. The owner of such a house must have been a person of some substance, a business man or merchant, or perhaps a retired centurion. As an indication of its size, it was at a later stage split into two separate houses, each still comparable in size with the majority of Vindolanda houses.

Next to the Corridor House are the remains of a strip house (about 30 x 10 feet), sub-divided into three rooms. A strip house is so-called because it occupies a narrow strip of land running back from the road—i.e., the building is end-on to the road rather than sideways-on in the modern fashion. It is noticeable that virtually all the other buildings follow the same pattern. The effect is to provide a greater number of buildings with access to the same length of road and, for shops and other establishments, to provide them with a frontage which is adequate for their business needs without the need to extend sideways for their domestic accommodation, which can be provided to the rear in the back part of the strip. Between the strip house and the west gate are the remains of two more buildings, likewise end-on to the road which may be shops, probably with accommodation at the rear, and possibly above

179

as well. These two buildings are almost exactly matched by two more on the opposite side of the road. Behind (i.e., to the south of) these is a row of buildings with their long axes east and west which appear to be aligned at the eastern ends. This suggests the existence of a *vicus* road running south from the west gate, parallel to the west rampart, with the buildings in the row placed end-on in relation to it, as on the main east-west road.

One other type of structure remains to be described, the building for the wives and children of married soldiers. These married quarters consist of two long, parallel blocks, again end-on to the road, just to the east of the stable block of the *mansio*. Each block is about 100 feet long and 20 feet wide, divided into rooms around 16 x 12 feet (one for each family), with a verandah in front. There may have been additional sleeping accommodation in a loft or small room above. Between them the two blocks provided space for about sixteen families, although there were probably other married quarters elsewhere in the *vicus*.

The visible buildings which have been described must be

Opposite: The replica stone Wall turret from within.

Below: The replica of the stone Wall and turret from the exterior. The Vindolanda complex includes full-scale replicas of portions of Hadrian's Wall, built between 1972 and 1974. The replica group includes a short section of Broad Wall (10 Roman feet wide), a typical turret (based on Brunton turret east of Chesters), a section of turf Wall with timber superstructure, a timber milecastle gateway, and a length of ditch on two sides of the group, c. 30 ft. wide and 8 ft. deep.

seen as only a sample of what originally existed. The *vicus* in its complete form must have included shops, bars and eating places, small manufacturing and trading establishments (for pottery, leatherwork, clothing etc.), storage or warehouse accommodation (there is a possible store-house to the west of the bath-house), married quarters for army wives and children, private houses for merchants, businessmen, retired soldiers etc. as well as, possibly, another inn, or another bathing establishment, together with other types of buildings for which there is at present no evidence.

South of the *vicus* is a complex of structures which are not ancient at all but which are of the greatest interest to anyone studying Hadrian's Wall. These are full-scale replicas (built 1972-4) of certain sections and features of the Wall. They consist of the ditch, a short section of stone wall, a turret, a short section of turf wall, with timber superstructure, and another section of turf wall, at right angles to the first, with a turf-and-timber milecastle gateway. These structures are grouped, for convenience, around three sides of a square in a way that they would never have been grouped on the Wall, but they nevertheless provide a most instructive supplement to any view of the visible remains of the frontier system. The stone (replica) turret, for example, conveys more vividly than any of the existing remains, what space there was inside the ground and first floor rooms; from the first floor one can go out onto the rampart walk of the (replica) section of Broad Wall and get something of the feeling of what it must have been like patrolling along the Wall from turret to turret. The turf wall replica illustrates one problem which must have faced the garrison troops, that of vegetation growing on the sloping faces of the rampart. Vegetation growth is indeed necessary to bind the surface together and inhibit erosion, but uncontrolled growth would have been both untidy and undesirable. At regular intervals, therefore, the vegetaion must have been trimmed back and this would have cleared the rampart faces of any unnecessary obstacle and at the same time would have promoted stronger growth and better roots to hold the surface firmly in place.

Complementing the structural remains visible on the ground are the collections in the site museum, most of them the result of the recent excavations. The museum is housed in Chesterholm, a house (of 1831) built mostly of Roman stones from Vindolanda itself, standing to the east of the fort just beyond Chaineley Burn. Among the wide range of finds are strong leather footwear, with studs, which would have been essential during the winter months, and writing tablets, including what is the earliest example of handwriting in Britain, around AD 100. Between them the museum collections and the visible structures make Vindolanda one of the most rewarding sites to visit along the Wall.

The Fort at South Shields

A fort in the Wall area not so far mentioned is the one at South Shields (Co. Durham), situated at the mouth of the Tyne, on the south bank, about four miles beyond Wallsend fort and the eastern end of the Wall. The existing remains date to the period of Septimius Severus (AD 193-211), but occupy the site of a fort apparently built in the time of Hadrian as part of the Wall system. A fort somewhere in this area would seem essential to a system which stopped some four miles short of the coast at Wallsend. Presumably the river was considered sufficient linear barrier (as on the European frontier), provided a watch could be kept over the end accessible from the sea—i.e., Tynemouth.

The fort measures 622 x 361 feet with four double gates in the standard position. As originally built it faced north-west. The surrounding stone wall was 6 feet thick and was backed by an earth rampart 16 feet wide. The whole fort was rebuilt early in the third century. The rebuilding, however, was not on the lines of a conventional auxiliary fort. First of all the

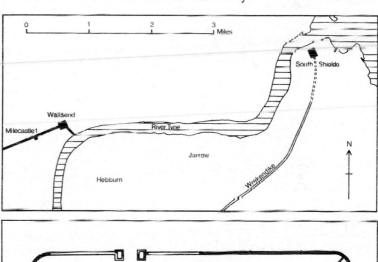

Map showing the relationship of the South Shields fort to the eastern end of the Wall at Wallsend.

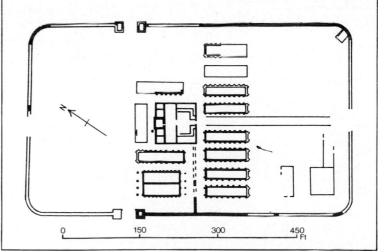

Plan of the fort at South Shields. Because it was a supply depot rather than a conventional fort the plan of South Shields is noticeably different from other forts. Much of its interior space was occupied by granaries. In addition to the twelve shown on the plan, another eight have been discovered in the rear portion of the fort.

orientation was changed, the new headquarters facing in the opposite direction, as at Vindolanda, so that the main entrance, the *porta praetoria*, was now on the south-east side. Of even greater interest were the other internal arrangements. A cross wall divided the interior into two more-or-less equal parts, south-eastern and north-western. The front wall of the headquarters was flush with the cross wall so that it could be reached only by the *via praetoria*. The other three entrances were in the north-western half of the fort.

The remaining buildings inside the fort consisted of granaries and barrack blocks with the main emphasis on the granaries. In the south-eastern part there was a row of eight granaries, end-on to the *via principalis*, each about 80 x 20 feet. The other buildings in this part were probably barrack blocks. In the north-western part there was an even larger group of granaries. The headquarters was flanked by a double and two single granaries, while in the rear portion of the fort there was another group of eight granaries, similar to the one in the *via principalis*. Thus, there are in all twenty granaries, far beyond the needs of a normal auxiliary unit for which, in any case, there would not now have been sufficient room. South Shields was not a normal auxiliary fort, whatever it started life as.

Its function and purpose are indicated by the nature of its internal buildings, by its position and by its date. The numerous granaries point clearly to its function as a supply base, a place where large quantities of basic food could be accumulated to serve the needs of a wide area or a large-scale campaign. Its position indicates how the grain was brought to 'South Shields, by sea, which in ancient times was the easiest method of transporting bulk cargoes. Finally, its date points to a part in whatever Septimius Severus was attempting to do in the period AD 208-210. In which role it must be considered in conjunction with Corbridge and its unusual range of buildings particularly the so-called storehouse. If South Shields was the specialized grain depot, then presumably the Corbridge depot was concerned with other types of supplies, complementary but equally essential to whatever undertaking was in progress. The road links of the Wall area to the south are clear and well-established. The South Shields depot points to an additional means of communication, by sea, specially suited to cargoes which it would have been very difficult to transport in sufficient quantity, even on the high quality roads which the Romans built for their military needs.

VIII

LOOKING AT THE WALL: YESTERDAY AND TODAY

SOLI
APOLLINI
ANICERO

The Venerable Bede (AD 672-735) is the first historian to mention the Wall in the post-Roman period, in his *Historia Ecclesiastica Gentis Anglorum*, where he actually quotes its dimensions as 8 feet thick and 12 feet high, the latter being the height to which it was still standing. It was not, however, until Elizabethan times, some 850 years later, that a sustained interest in the Wall and its place in English history began. The first important work containing information on the subject was that of William Campden, the great Elizabethan antiquary. His *Britannia* (5th edition, 1600), written in Latin, was translated into English in 1610 and went through many editions during the next two centuries, the last one appearing in 1806, new information on the Wall having been added from time to time. The later editions (1789, 1806) were based on another notable work, John Horsley's *Britannia Romana* (1732), which was a careful study not only of Hadrian's Wall but of Roman Britain as a whole. Two other works drawing heavily on Horseley's account are Gordon's *Itinerarium Septentrionale* (1726 — i.e., using Horsley's as yet unpublished material), and Warburton's *Vallum Romanum* (1753).

Another great English antiquary, William Stukeley, published his *Iter Boreale* in 1776. One of the most useful aspects of this work was that it contained drawings showing the state of the Wall at the time, which can be compared with their present state. The *History of Newcastle* (1789) by John Brand also contained an account of the Wall. Other works around this time are William Hutton's *History of the Roman Wall* (1802), Daniel and Samuel Lyson's fourth volume of *Magna Britannia* (1816), and John Hodgson's *Picture of Newcastle upon Tyne* (1812). However, Hodgson made his greatest contribution in a later work, the last volume of his *History of Northumberland* (1839), which dealt with both the Hadrianic and Antonine Walls. Hodgson treated the Wall proper and the Vallum as part of the same scheme, which we now know to be true; previously they had been regarded as two separate frontiers, the Vallum being attributed to Hadrian and the Wall to Severus.

The middle of the nineteenth century saw two important publications. In 1851 John Collingwood Bruce published the first edition of his *Roman Wall*, followed by two other editions in 1853 and 1867. A by-product of this was the famous *Handbook to the Roman Wall* which was first published in 1863 and which has gone through numerous editions and reprintings up to the present day. The second major publication was *A Survey of the Roman Wall* (1858), by Henry MacLauchlan, which contained the first accurate and detailed survey of the Wall, carried out in the years 1852-4. In the latter part of the nineteenth century and in the twentieth the bulk of the work on Hadrian's Wall has been published in the journals of two northern Societies: *Archaeologia Aeliana*, the

Overleaf: An early view of the Wall at Steel Rig, about 2 miles west of Housesteads.

journal of the *Society of Antiquaries of Newcastle upon Tyne*, and the *Transactions of the Cumberland and Westmorland Archaeological and Antiquarian Society*.

The Pilgrimages

A unique feature in the study of Hadrian's Wall are the so-called pilgrimages which have taken place at regular intervals since the first one in 1849. This was organized by John Collingwood Bruce, mentioned earlier as the author of the famous *Handbook to the Roman Wall*, and the nature and intention of these pilgrimages can be best understood from the quotation below from a paper by Bruce. At the end of a course of lectures on the Wall in the winter of 1848-9, he stated: 'I had endeavoured by pictorial representation and verbal description to show its present condition, but that if any of them would like to examine it for themselves I should be glad to accompany them in the following summer in traversing it from end to end—forming a pilgrimage like that described by Chaucer, consisting of both ladies and gentlemen.'

To this may be added Eric Birley's comment on the same passage: 'The last sentence reveals the character of the excursion. It was a social, gossiping affair, its participants ready to take as much interest in "the beauty of the country to be traversed and the attractive features which it presents to the botanist and the geologist" (to quote from the programme

An early view of the Wall and Castle Nick milecastle. (No. 39).

which Bruce issued) as in the Roman remains; and as far as the remains are concerned, it was their appearance rather than their historial significance that attracted most attention.' Occasionally the pilgrims went hunting for Roman antiquities and occasionally they did a little digging, for example, in the west postern gate at Birdoswald. Bruce addressed the pilgrims informally as required, but also more formally addressed larger audiences who gathered at various points from the surrounding neighbourhood.

The first pilgrimage in 1849 was organized by John Collingwood Bruce on a private basis. The second pilgrimage was not until 1886 and was on a more formal basis, organized jointly by the *Cumberland and Westmorland Archaeological and Antiquarian Society* and the *Society of Antiquaries of Newcastle upon Tyne*, in honour of Bruce, who was by then eighty-one and the doyen of Wall studies. As a result of the great success of the second pilgrimage it was suggested that they should become a regular feature of Wall studies.

Bruce died in 1892 and the third pilgrimage took place in 1896, ten years after the previous one, followed by the fourth in 1906. For obvious reasons the fifth pilgrimage did not take in 1916 but was deferred until 1920. This was followed by the sixth pilgrimage in 1930 and should have been followed by the seventh in 1940, but again for obvious reasons, it had to be deferred until a later date. It was eventually decided to hold

An early view of the Wall ditch (between Carvoran and Birdoswald).

the seventh pilgrimage in 1949, the centenary of the first one organized privately by Bruce in 1849. The eighth pilgrimage followed ten years later in 1959 and the ninth in turn in 1969, the most recent of the series. The tenth pilgrimage will take place in 1979.

As can well be imagined the nature of the pilgrimages has changed somewhat since the early ones in the nineteenth century. Attention is now focussed much more closely on the Wall itself and on the problems thrown up by the excavations at various sites along the Wall. The ten year intervals between pilgrimages mean that an enormous amount of new information has to be reported and discussed and the six days of the meeting (Monday to Saturday) are a very busy time for pilgrims. The often splendid scenery is no doubt enjoyed, but there is equally no doubt now about the primary objective of the pilgrimages: the serious study of Hadrian's Wall and all its attendant problems, albeit in the most pleasurable circumstances, out of doors with the monument in full view.

What to see on the Wall

Inevitably, Housesteads, Chesters, Vindolanda, Birdoswald, Corbridge and South Shields must loom large in visits to Hadrian's Wall. For many people the Wall forts are the only part of the system they ever see, and more often than not their visits are concentrated on Housesteads and/or Chesters, although the current excavations at Vindolanda have attracted a large number of visitors. However, it should now be clear that there is a great deal more than can easily be seen and it would be a great pity if any examination of the Wall was confined to the auxiliary forts. They are certainly an essential part of the picture, but the picture will be just as incomplete if the milecastles, turrets etc. are left out as if the forts themselves were not seen. The various sites and features listed below provide a representative sample of all parts of the Wall system.

But before dealing with these one other aspect of the Wall should be mentioned—museums. With the exception of Birdoswald, the accessible forts at Housesteads, Chesters, Vindolanda, Corbridge and South Shields are provided with excellent site museums, housing many of the finds produced by excavation and so complementing the picture presented by the standing structural remains. The finds are accompanied by written information, maps, models etc. aimed at re-creating the life of the fort, both in its everyday aspect and its historical aspect, as a structure occupied for nearly three hundred years along an important frontier. In the same context can be mentioned the two major museums in the area which contain large amounts of material from the Wall. These are the Tullie House Museum in Carlisle and the University

Museum, Newcastle-upon-Tyne. These two collections, together with those in the site museums mentioned already, balance the wide range of structural remains to be found along the Wall and are an essential part of any comprehensive view of the frontier system in all its aspects.

Before dealing with milecastles, two other forts along the Wall can be mentioned. The six sites dealt with above all have substantial excavated remains, left exposed for the visitor. Carrawbrough (5 miles to the east of Housesteads), and Great Chesters (6 miles to the west), however, although some excavation has been carried out there (and filled in again), are both in what may be termed their natural state. They exist and are clearly visible as earthworks, grass-covered banks and ditches defining the size and shape of the fort, even if they show little or nothing of the internal features. They provide a useful corrective to the impression given by the excavated forts and are well worth seeing. At Carrawbrough the size of the earthworks indicates very substantial remains of ramparts and gates. Great Chesters occupies the site of milecastle 43 which had to be pulled down to make way for it. Like Housesteads it is side-on to the Wall) i.e., its *porta praetoria* faces east), while on the west side are the remains of no less than four parallel outer ditches.

There is an additional reason for visiting Carrawbrough. In 1949 a small temple of Mithras, originally a Persian god whose cult was popular with the army, was discovered just to the south-west of the fort. The temple, stone-built, measures 43 x 18 feet and was built early in the third century AD. At the north-western end are three altars, although these have now been replaced by replicas, the originals being in the museum in Newcastle, where there is a replica of the site. There is also a small model of the site in Housesteads museum.

After the forts come the milecastles, the fortlets placed at every Roman mile along the Wall and numbered from east to west (i.e., numbered by us for convenience, not by the Romans). A number of these have been mentioned already. Harrow's Scar (milecastle 49, long axis) is within a few minutes walk of Birdoswald and must be included in any visit there, particularly as this involves walking beside an excellent stretch of the Wall and obtaining, from the milecastle, an excellent view over the River Irthing crossing and the stretch of Wall beyond to the east. Milecastle 37 (short axis) is the same sort of distance to the west of Housesteads, and again must be included in a visit there, particularly as this involves walking along a stretch of Wall which stands dramatically above steep crags where an outer ditch would have been completely superfluous, if not impossible to dig.

Two other milecastles which ought to be seen are Cawfields and Poltross Burn. Cawfields (milecastle 42) is about three-quarters of a mile to the east of Great Chesters and is only a

Brunton turret to the east of Chesters.

few minutes walk from a convenient car park, reached by a signposted side road on the north side of the B6318 at Haltwhistle Burn, about four miles east of the junction with the A69 at Greenhead. The milecastle is of the short axis type, and its walls are preserved to a height of three or four feet. Poltross Burn (milecastle 48) is of the long axis type and the remains of its two internal barrack blocks, as of most of its ramparts, are well preserved. It is signposted from the road through Gilsland village (the B6318), about two miles west of Greenhead.

If further examples of the milecastle type are required then there are Castle Nick (milecastle 39, long axis), on the high crags about two miles west of Housesteads; milecastles 32 and 33, by the road, the B6318, threequarters, and one and threequarters of a mile west of Carrawbrough respectively; and milecastle 23 on the B6318 about four miles west of Chollerford Bridge near Chesters.

Banks East turret on the road running west from Birdoswald.

More than a dozen turrets are preserved at various points along the Wall, half a dozen of them in the Birdoswald region. Turret 49b is on the road edge only a quarter of a mile west of the fort, which is linked to it by a stretch of Wall, with only a short break just east of the turret. There are three other turrets (51a, 51b and 52a) further along the road to the west, between one a half and two and a half miles from Birdoswald. There are long stretches of Wall ditch along this road, on the north side, with equally long stretches of vallum to the south. Two other turrets, 48a and 48b can be seen in association with the visit to the Willowford Bridge abutment on the east bank of the River Irthing (below).

Two more turrets (44b and 45a) are situated at the western end of the high crags sector and are perhaps less readily accessible than those near Birdoswald. Another turret (41a) is located just over half a mile to the east of Cawfields milecastle (above), and can be seen at the same time by continuing

*The turret on Sewingshields Crags
during the course of excavation.*

eastwards along the Wall which is preserved for just under half
a mile here. Further east, turret 35a, about a mile to the east
of Housesteads, is, like 44b and 45a, rather less easy of access
than some others. Further east again, in the area of
Carrawbrough and Chesters are two more easily accessible
turrets, 29a and 26b. Turret 29a, attached to a short section of
Wall, is just north of the road (B6318), about two miles west of
Chesters, while 26b is about half a mile to the east. Other
surviving turrets are 33b, 34a and 7b, the latter on the western
outskirts of Newcastle upon Tyne.

Some well-preserved sections of Wall, frontal ditch and
vallum, have been mentioned already. Apart from these the
longest stretches of surviving Wall are in the high crags
section, from Housesteads in the east to Carvoran in the west,
a distance of some nine miles, although the Wall is not
continuous for the whole of this length. Nevertheless, allowing
for the gaps, there are about five miles of Wall preserved to

195

varying heights in this section. To the rear of this stretch of Wall are long stretches of vallum, many of them with the crossings provided when Hadrian's Wall was superseded by the Antonine Wall. In some places the vallum is up to half a mile back from the Wall, at the foot of the slope down from the cliff-edge to the north. In addition to the long stretch of ditch to the west of Birdoswald there is another considerable stretch, again immediately north of the road (B6318) from the point where the latter converges with the Wall, at turret 33b, eastwards for about five miles, with only one or two breaks, nearly as far as Chesters. There is another three-mile section to the east of Chesters, again immediately north of the road.

One or two other more specialized features can be fitted in with the visits suggested so far. The eastern abutment for the bridge which carried the Wall across the North Tyne can be seen on the visit to Chesters, although it cannot be reached directly from the fort which is on the other side of the river. The approach is via a footpath along the river bank from the modern bridge at Chollerford, about half a mile east of Chesters. Similarly the eastern abutment of the bridge across the River Irthing can be seen when visiting Birdoswald, although again it is not directly accessible from the fort. It can be seen at a distance, from above, from Harrow's Scar mile-castle, but then one must go back to Birdoswald and from there to Gilsland Village about two miles by road, where there is a signpost (near the school) to the remains. They include not only the bridge abutment and an associated tower, but also two turrets (48a and 48b), and a good stretch of narrow Wall, built on a broad Wall foundation.

Two other features not so far mentioned in the book should also be included in any programme of visits. These are the vallum causeway and gate and the temple at Benwell in Newcastle upon Tyne. The vallum causeway and gate is the only surviving example along the Wall of the access arrangements of this feature of the system. It consists of the causeway across the vallum ditch (about 37 x 42 feet), with stone revetted sides and the remains of the stonework for the gateway across the middle of the causeway, the gates opening inwards—i.e. towards the fort, from which access was controlled. Nearby, in Broombridge Avenue, are the remains of another small Roman temple, to Antenociticus, an obscure god, whose cult was possibly brought in by the first cohort of Vangiones who garrisoned Benwell fort in the second century.

The sites mentioned in the preceding paragraphs provide a representative and mostly easily accessible sample of the various features of the Wall system. It is noticeable that they are, with only a few exceptions, in the central sector of the Wall, between the Chesters area and that of Birdoswald, a distance of about twenty-five miles. Apart from the sites already mentioned there is not a great deal to see in the

Turret at East Denton on the western outskirts of Newcastle-upon-Tyne.

A stretch of surviving Wall at Heddon on the Wall, about seven miles west of Newcastle.

Above: The Vallum crossing at Benwell (restored).

Imaginative reconstruction of the Vallum crossing and gateway.

Remains of the Roman temple at Benwell.

eastern sector of the Wall, and even less in the western sector, although quite a lot is known in both sectors as a result of excavation. Certainly the line of the Wall and the position of most milecastles and turrets is well established. A visit to South Shields will make clear the tactical position at the east coast end of the system. Although there is virtually nothing to see west of Carlisle, a visit to the west coast area around Bowness will nevertheless help to make clear the problems the Romans faced in trying to protect one side of the wide Solway estuary.

In the context of visits to Hadrian's Wall it is appropriate to say something about useful aids, apart from general books on the Wall as a whole. John Collingwood Bruce's *Handbook to the Roman Wall*, which has gone through many editions and revisions, is still extremely useful although inevitably now out of date in certain places. Nevertheless, it gives a vast amount of information which cannot easily be obtained elsewhere. Apart from this the most useful aids as far as field trips are concerned are maps. The whole of the Wall area is covered by sheets of the Ordnance Surveys One-inch and One-and-a-

199

quarter inch maps, but by far the most useful single source of information is the special Ordance Survey *Map of Hadrian's Wall*, at a scale of two inches to one mile. This shows the whole of the Wall system, superimposed on a modern map, and differentiates between visible remains (in black) and remains known but not visible (red). It is an indispensable aid to any sort of work on the Wall, be it casual visit or serious research. It is quite invaluable in planning trips to the visible features of the Wall and equally useful as a comprehensive picture of the system for the purpose of reading and contemplation.

Summary

After outlining the main facts about Hadrian's Wall and highlighting some of the problems, it becomes clear that the evidence, both geographically and historically, is patchy. Although there has been a great deal of excavation along the frontier, the full story of the majority of forts has yet to be extracted, and until this has been done we cannot begin to write a comprehensive account of the Wall system. The conclusions drawn from the excavated forts in the central sector of the Wall may not hold good for the forts in the eastern and western sectors. The Wall is the sum total of its parts and undoubtedly the most important parts are the auxiliary forts; until we know a great deal more about some of them we cannot expect the answer to the sum to be particularly accurate.

The history of the Wall is equally patchy. As far as we know, it can be summarized by a dozen or so dates: AD 122, 139, 155, 181, 197, 296, 343, 367, 383, 397, 406, and 410. Even allowing for the events which followed these years, there are still very large blanks in a story which extended in all for nearly three hundred years. The assumption is that if nothing was recorded then all was quiet along the frontier and the Wall was doing the job it was intended to do. But more positive evidence is needed for a true historical account of the Wall. Britain was a remote province and probably did not occupy a prominent place in the consciousness of Roman historians. Major events might be recorded, but only briefly, and minor happenings completely ignored, particularly if there were more important developments in or near Rome at the time. The chances are that many happenings along the Wall have no historical record at all. The full story will have to be written from the evidence provided by the Wall itself. Only when much more is known about the history of the separate sites will it be possible to fill in some gaps in the existing accounts of the Wall as a whole. If what has been said in these paragraphs appears to contradict the apparently large amount of knowledge outlined in the earlier chapters, then it is perhaps some indication of what the picture could be, given the will and the resources to rectify the situation. The recent suggestions that Hadrian's Wall could accommodate many more visitors if its full extent was exploited is perhaps a pointer to what may happen in the future. Hopefully, Housesteads and a few other sites may not always have to bear the brunt of summer visitors. A much wider choice is needed, for both practical and academic reasons.

The final word in a book such as this must be an exhortation to go and see it for oneself. No amount of writing, no matter how well illustrated, is quite the same as seeing the monument on the ground. Its military function is long since gone but Hadrian's Wall is still performing yeoman service as a spotlight on an important aspect of Britain's Roman past.

BIBLIOGRAPHY

BIRLEY, E.,   *Research on Hadrian's Wall,* T. Wilson and Son Ltd., Kendal, 1961.

BIRLEY, E.,   *Chesters Roman Fort,* D.O.E. Official Guidebook, 1973.

BIRLEY, E.,   *Housesteads Roman Fort,* D.O.E. Official Guidebook, 1975.

BIRLEY, E.,   *Corbridge Roman Station,* D.O.E. Official Guidebook, 1975.

BIRLEY, R.,   *Hadrian's Wall, Central Sector,* Northern History Booklet, No. 19, F. Graham, Newcastle, 1972.

BIRLEY, R.,   *Vindolanda Roman Fort, Civilian Settlement,* Barcombe Publications, Haltwhistle, Northumberland, 1976.

BREEZE, D. J., and   *Hadrian's Wall,* Allen Lane, London, 1976.
DOBSON, B.,

BRUCE, J. C.,   *The Roman Wall,* Newcastle, 1851.

BRUCE, J. C., and   *Handbook to the Roman Wall* (12th ed.), 1966.
RICHMOND, I. A.,

COLLINGWOOD, R. G., *The Archaeology of Roman Britain,* Methuen, London, 1969.
and RICHMOND, I. A.,

DAVIES, H.,   *A Walk Along the Wall,* Quartet Books, London, 1974.

DIVINE, D.,   *The North-West Frontier of Rome,* Macdonald, London, 1969.

DURANT, G. M.,   *Britain, Rome's Most Northerly Province,* Bell, London, 1969.

FRERE, S.S.,   *Britannia: A History of Roman Britain,* Routledge and Kegan Paul, London, 1967.

HOWARD, P.,   *Birdoswald Fort on Hadrian's Wall,* Northern History Booklet, No. 73, F. Graham, Newcastle, 1976.

JONES, G. D. B.,   *Hadrian's Wall from the Air,* Archaeological Surveys Ltd., 1976.

RICHMOND, I. A.,   *Roman Britain,* Penguin Books, 1955.

WILSON, D. R.,   *Roman Frontiers of Britain,* Heinemann Regional Archaeologies, London, 1967. ·

INDEX